Stuffed

To Robyn-
u know you appreciate
Al + Linda's H.E. collection
personally.

xxx,
Nana

Stuffed

Emptying the Hoarder's Nest
A True Tale

Nona Smith

Stuffed
Emptying the Hoarder's Nest
Copyright © 2014 Nona Smith

P.O. Box 1778, Mendocino, CA 95460

Summary: This is the sometimes melancholy, sometimes humorous story of a non-hoarder's journey helping dismantle the estate of two eclectic hoarders.

ISBN: 978-0-9914879-0-5

Cover photograph © Nona Smith
Cover design: Cypress House
Book production by Cypress House

Printed in the United States of America
First Printing, 2014
246897531

Behind all this,
some great happiness is hiding.
— Yehuda Amichai

Contents

Stuffed

I don't possess a hoarding gene. I own no workbench piled high with broken items I might someday get around to fixing. I don't save that one earring hoping its missing twin will turn up. No clothes linger in my closet waiting for fashion to return them to vogue. Books I've read get passed along. I even clean out my recipe files.

My husband Art and I used to watch the television show *Hoarders.* Like a rubber-necker at the scene of an accident, I was curious about what happened to those people and their stuff, but I never related to them.

Some of my friends are hoarders---intelligent, reasonable people, who collect things: empty boxes, articles from newspapers, silver trays inherited from great aunts that take up closet space and never get used. I don't do that. Which is why I didn't suspect hoarding could become a problem for me.

I was wrong.

Thirty months ago my husband's friend Linda died, leaving Art the trustee of her estate, including the remains of her late husband's trust. In the eight years since Al's death, Linda changed nothing. Sold nothing. Gave nothing away. Not his clothing. Not the stocks they'd purchased in a better economy. Not subscriptions to magazines he could no longer read.

Art knew the couple collected things. He'd been in the apartment building they owned. He was aware that except for one rent-paying tenant, the rest of the two-bedroom apartments overflowed with his friends' stuff. He'd seen the condition of the basement. He knew about the computer repair shop. The warehouse in Albany. The two houses in southern California. But not until he became responsible for all of it did he fully grasp the situation.

We stood together in the living room of the apartment the couple shared for decades, and I turned to Art. "You knew about this?"

"Yeah," he said. He sounded stunned and looked around as if seeing the place for the first time. "But I didn't think they'd die."

We took in the chaos: hundreds of stuffed animals (mostly teddy bears), computer screens and keyboards in various states of repair and disrepair, tools of every kind, mechanical musical machines. We saw apothecary jars, botanical prints, Navajo rugs and jewelry-making equipment. In the kitchen, first-print coin sets crammed a cabinet under the stove, unopened coke bottles from the 1950s and glass paperweights that looked like objects d'art filled the cupboards. In one bedroom, the closet shelves over-flowed with antique metal toys. A large collection of flashlights crowded the closet floor. Scattered around the room, we found old radios and rusty cooking implements amid boxes of unsharpened pencils and dozens of still-pinned-and-folded, never worn plaid shirts. A hall closet swelled with table linens for parties they'd never hosted. In Linda's bedroom, sweet hand-pinched, clay animals lined the shelves, and teddy bears were everywhere.

Some of the items we knew were rare and valuable; some had been improperly stored and lost whatever value they might have had. Moths had eaten sections of the Navajo rugs. Dampness bled one botanical print into another. Many items were duplicated and in their original packaging: sets of stainless stacking bowls, rolls of thirty-five millimeter film, cartons of Scotch tape, twenty CDs of *The Sound of Music*. Two hefty, sealed cardboard boxes from England bearing the Steiff label held sizeable twin teddy bears, tucked away like Sleeping Beauty.

We walked through the four apartments, assaying their contents, trying to make sense of where to start dissembling this estate. After two hours, we ended up back in Linda's apartment where the teddy bears occupied all the best seats.

"This creeps me out," I said, wrinkling my nose.

"No kidding." Art looked downcast as he ushered me out and locked the door.

That night, I couldn't sleep. Finally, I left our warm bed, sat at the computer, and Googled "hoarders." On the Mayo Clinic site I read that hoarding, "the excessive collection of items along with the inability to discard them," falls on the spectrum of obsessive-compulsive disorder. A section of the brain called the anterior cingulate controls decision-making, problem solving, and spatial orientation. It operates differently in the hoarder than in the average person. Understanding that hoarding is a compulsion was a great relief to me, and I was pleased there was no blame involved. It wasn't anyone's *fault* they hoarded, but rather a dysfunction of their anterior cingulate.

I understand compulsions. Mine run toward organizing, putting like items together and in place, throwing out useless stuff. In fact, I could imagine that *my* compulsion would enable me to effectively work with theirs. I slipped back into bed and had no trouble falling asleep.

The next morning I felt full of energy and enthusiasm. "Hey," I said to Art. "I get it now, and I know where we'll begin."

Art looked up from behind his coffee cup, waiting for me to continue.

"First, we'll sort the teddy bears for sale and donation. Then we'll locate all the Navajo rugs and move them to a single room so we can get to the glass paperweights and apothecary jars and box them up. This will give us room to maneuver the mechanical musical instruments into the open to be viewed for appraisal."

I was on it.

The Plan

Who were these people whose stuff would consume the next two years of our lives? They were the Nielsens, Al and Linda. Art and Al shared a friendship spanning forty years.

"He's a Renaissance man," Art told me years before I met Al. "He taught elementary school. But before that, he was a train engineer. He also piloted planes. He's an accomplished pianist, a computer guru, and a brilliant photographer. He makes jewelry and repairs antique musical instruments like player pianos and calliopes. He collects coins and invests in commodities. I believe he knows something about everything."

I was disappointed when I finally met Al, who turned out to be an overweight, glad-handing guy in a plaid shirt with coke-bottle-thick glasses. I'd been imagining a latter day Michelangelo.

Linda was another surprise. I knew she had Multiple Sclerosis (MS) and was wheelchair-bound, but I'd pictured her a kind of female version of her husband: outgoing, jolly. Instead, she was soft-spoken, timid and retiring. Her blue eyes lacked twinkle; strands of limp, gray hair framed her face.

The couple had been devastated when Linda was first diagnosed a decade earlier. Western medicine had little to offer in the way of help or hope; the only assistance they found was in palliative care and support groups. So Al and Linda devised their own plan for dealing with her illness. *Their* plan involved the Hemlock Society and hoarding medication. Hoarding was not a new concept to them.

As Linda's illness progressed, their lives grew incrementally smaller. She seldom left the apartment. Al became her sole caretaker. Friends were no longer invited in. They abandoned house cleaning, and Linda stopped cooking, although she continued to watch the Food Network channel, which was on whenever Art visited them.

Their exit plan was in place the morning Al slipped in the shower and hit his head on the floor. It was still in place two days later when he died, leaving Linda alone with bottles of medication she could no longer open.

In the weeks that followed, Art helped Linda cope with her new reality. He found a case manager to deal with her daily physical needs. He helped her hire a lawyer to resolve Al's estate, and an accountant to deal with her finances. He took upon himself the supervision of her real estate holdings, made sure her chair lift was operational, her handicapped van serviced, and that she had transportation to her medical appointments. He'd made Al a promise to look after Linda, and he would keep his word, as faithfully as Linda would allow it.

She became obsessed with keeping everything the way it was before Al died. Almost immediately, a problem arose when her medical insurance company insisted she update her Advanced Medical Care Directive. They wanted her to name someone more available than Al to take charge of her health decisions if she couldn't make them for herself. When their administrative offices were unable to get Linda to cooperate, a social worker appealed to Art.

"I think Linda feels more comfortable with women," Art said to me. "Will you work with her on this?"

I visited Linda on a chilly morning, two months after Al's death. A home care aide let me in, and I threaded my way through a narrow path of furniture and boxes to Linda's bedroom. Drapes were drawn against the weak winter sun. Linda sat in bed, propped by pillows, and watched Rachel Ray on the Food Network Channel prepare a mouth-watering macaroni and cheese casserole.

Moving aside teddy bears, I perched on the edge of the bed and reached for the new directive on her bedside table. She struggled with the mute button on the TV remote, but I'd learned not to offer help unless she asked for it. Her dignity was at stake, and I respected that.

Shelves, filled with a collection of teddy bears, ran the length and breadth of the bedroom. Bears in coats and muffs, warm sweaters and pants, hiking outfits and tutus. They spilled over her dresser and onto her bed.

A Hoyle lift dangled from the ceiling above her, chrome and gleaming. Mornings, with the help of an aide, the contraption lifted her body out of bed and into her wheelchair. Nights, it deposited her back.

"Ready?" I asked when she'd settled back against the pillows. She nodded.

"Kaiser wants to know about your wishes should you no longer be able to communicate your own needs. Do you want heroic measures taken to preserve your life?"

"No." sShe shook her head.

"Do you want to be put on life support systems?"

Another emphatic *no*.

"Do you want your life preserved if you can no longer interact with family and friends?"

A tear trembled at the corner of her eye. She struggled to wipe it with her sleeve, but couldn't raise her hand to her face. I took a tissue from my pocket and dabbed at the tear, then skipped the next question, which asked what she would want if she could no longer dress, feed or take care of her own bodily functions.

On TV, Rachel silently ladled the mac and cheese onto plates, garnishing each with thin, crispy onions.

We finished the directive and I folded Linda's stiff fingers around a pen. Together, we wrote her signature, which looked more like my handwriting than hers. Then we sat amongst her teddy bears and watched Rachel concoct an apple cobbler.

In the years that followed, we visited Linda frequently, bringing her the outside world through stories and photographs of trips we'd taken. She had few visitors other than her health care aides, a bookkeeper, and her friend Hanae.

As time passed, her physical condition worsened. She could no longer operate her electric wheelchair, her voice became a whisper, and her breathing labored.

Seven years from the day we filled out her new Advanced Care Directive, Art received a call from Kaiser Hospital. Linda was in Intensive Care. He needed to come as soon as possible.

When we arrived we found Linda, skeletal and waxy-faced. Her thin, grey hair was matted against a pillow, her eyes slits. Feeding and breathing tubes snaked out of her mouth. Round, plastic disks, attached to a breathing apparatus, sucked her cheeks in and out, in and out. She stared blankly at the silent television where Rachel was preparing Thanksgiving dinner.

Where was that health care directive?

Hanae greeted us with a concerned frown. The lights were dim and the room smelled of hospital. Two of Linda's aides huddled near the window, heads together, rosaries swaying. We waited for the doctor to arrive.

When he came, the five of us stood, mute witnesses, as he explained Linda's condition to her.

"You have an infection in your lungs, which are very weak from MS. You can't breathe on your own, so we've installed a respirator to breathe for you. You have a severe bladder infection and a high fever. We can't take your breathing tubes out, but if you want to communicate, nod your head for yes, and shake it for no. Do you understand?"

Linda did not move.

He leaned closer. "Did you understand what I said? If you do, please blink once."

She blinked. He took that for assent.

"Do you want us to take extreme measures to keep you alive?"

Another blink.

"Do you want to continue to live even if you need a breathing tube to stay alive?"

Linda blinked again.

"Do you want us to take extreme measures to keep you alive even if you can't communicate with family and friends?"

Blink.

"Do you understand that means you will need to remain hospitalized?"

I was aghast. This was against everything Linda and Al planned, against her own wishes in her most recent directive. *Where was that paper Kaiser was so insistent she update? Why was she hooked up to these machines? How did this happen?*

Out in the hall, away from the others, Art and I spoke to the doctor.

"Do you have Linda's Health Care Directive?"

He leafed through her thick medical file. "I do."

"Then how could this happen?"

He shrugged his shoulders. "I was prepared for another scenario myself when I came today."

"Is it possible MS is affecting her thinking?" I asked.

"It's quite possible, but we can't prove it. We must obey the patient's wishes if they're able to communicate them. It's the law."

A rustling in her room drew us back to find Linda looking more alert but agitated. She moaned, the breathing tube disabled her speech.

"She wants to go home," one of the aides said.

The doctor leaned toward Linda. "That's not possible while you still need the breathing machine."

Exhausted from her efforts, Linda's head rolled back against the pillows.

The doctor put his hand on Linda's arm, gave it a squeeze and departed. He had nothing further to offer. Hanae, Art and I stood helpless in the face of hospital policy and "the law."

Over the next two days, Linda's condition deteriorated. She continued to be agitated, rasping over and over her request to go home. One doctor finally took pity on her and signed her release. With breathing tubes and ventilator still in place, an ambulance, its sirens silenced, brought Linda home.

There she passed her final hours, surrounded by her beloved teddy bears and soothed by Rachel Ray's voice.

Somewhere in that apartment waited a stash of hoarded pills, their "discard by" dates expired.

Channeling Linda

Two weeks after Linda died, we stood at the door of her apartment, key hovering at the lock. We felt like trespassers.

Art gave a small shrug, turned the key, and pushed the door open. Dust motes and stale air greeted us. I felt a familiar tickle at the back of my throat, the one I always felt when we came here: an irritation caused by dust, mold and mildew. I coughed.

Stepping across the threshold, we stood in the living room. Two oak desks sat side by side in front of the draped windows. On one were Linda's computer, printer, shredder and phone. Old mail, catalogues and file boxes buried the other. Drawers exploded with writing implements, pads, a stockpile of staplers and scotch tape equal to any quantity found at Office Depot.

Tall, black stereo speakers dominated the far wall, bracketing a mammoth CD player. Art laid a hand on one. "Al told me this piece of equipment can hold a hundred CDs at one time."

I raised my eyebrows. "They owned a hundred CDs?"

He gestured to a six-foot tall, four sided cabinet in the corner, packed with an eclectic collection of music: country-western, classical, jazz, ragtime, folk singers from the 1950s, popular music of the American Bandstand era, and five shelves devoted entirely to Christmas music.

"I see. More than a hundred," I murmured.

Except for a wheelchair folded against the wall, a faux leather armchair was the only visible seating in the room. It reclined, in blue splendor, in front of the speakers.

On the adjacent wall, two Tiffany-replica floor lamps with gem colored shades stood like sentinels on either side of a large mound of stuffed animals. Looking at that soft, dusty heap made my throat tighten. I coughed again.

More teddy bears, monkeys, pigs and lambs covered the coffee table in front of the mountain.

We peered into the dining room and kitchen.

"Did you ever eat here?" I asked Art.

"Never. Where would I sit?"

Al had commandeered the dining room for one of his hobbies. Three workbenches, laden with jewelry-making equipment and supplies, stood in place of a dining room table and chairs.

"They ate a lot of take out. I don't know when they *ever* cooked in the kitchen. Have a look."

The kitchen counters were lined with packages of paper plates and straws, large apothecary jars and unopened kitchen gadgets, flashlights, boxes filled with costume jewelry and empty canisters. Everything was covered with a layer of grime. My throat constricted.

I shook my head. "Was it *always* like this?"

There was no judgment in Art's voice. "Ever since I've known them," he said.

Alice must have felt like this on her way down that rabbit hole. "Theirs was a different reality, wasn't it?"

He nodded and looked sad.

As we headed toward the bedrooms we passed a miniature, artificial Christmas tree perched on an aluminum TV tray and festooned with tiny ornaments.

Art nodded in the direction of the tree. "That's been here, Christmas and Easter, winter and spring, for years."

From the hall, we glanced into the second bedroom. Piled high on a daybed were teddy bears, cases of medical supplies, a brass trumpet and an accumulation of women's purses. Al's clothes shared the closet with cases of adult diapers, several folded Navajo rugs, and dozens of cameras. More teddy bears and assorted stuffed animals congregated on the closet shelf, along with empty boxes. Two wicker doll carriages were parked under a window. One held a jar of mystery keys. An old mattress leaned against the wall, and a life-size bear slouched in the corner.

Cough. Cough.

The bathroom was situated between the two bedrooms and passing it reminded me why I always came to visit Linda with an empty bladder.

We entered her bedroom, and although I expected to, I didn't have a sense of her presence. Bottles of medicine still filled her bedside table, the Hoyle lift dangled above her bed. Teddy bears lined the walls and spilled over onto her headboard and dresser. They seemed to be waiting patiently for what was to come next.

But Linda was no longer here. I had a feeling she'd moved on. This was where we decided to begin our work. Here, in apartment number five, where Al and Linda started their life together and accumulated stuff that eventually spilled into three other apartments, a store, a warehouse, and two houses in southern California.

Apartment number five was besieged with stuffed animals and Linda's teddy bears that sat on, paraded over, drooped upon and slumped against every flat surface. A plentitude of bears lived in the other apartments as well.

In addition to more teddy bears, the other properties also stored player pianos, calliopes, zithers, organ grinders, and paper musical scrolls wound around wooden spools. Duplicate tools of all manner and kind. Original signed and numbered Henry Evans botanical linoleum block prints. Glass-printed apothecary jars and medicine bottles. Coins. Clothing from relatives long dead. Stashes of empty perfume bottles. Commodore computers, screens, and keyboards. A six-foot-long, wooden slide rule. De-accessioned books from the school library where Linda worked. One hundred-twenty pair of white, cotton socks in their original packages. Plymouths. From 1957. Six of them, stored in the carport.

A cloud of overwhelm loomed above us as we stood in Linda's bedroom.

Art reached out and touched my shoulder. "Thanks for helping me with this."

"Well, actually, I was thinking about going out for a massage and picking you up again around 5:00." I smiled.

But he was in no mood for humor. "I'll tackle the desk and file drawers in the living room. Why don't you see if you can make some headway in here?"

I knew nothing about collectible teddy bears. But someone had to deal with them, if only to get them out of the way to access the things they obscured.

I stood for a moment and looked around. Drapes covered the sliding glass doors running the length of the room and a triple-tiered shelf stood in front of them. The shelf sagged in the middle from bear weight. Sunshine had eaten the curtains, and some of the bears were wedged between the decaying material and the back of the shelf.

I couldn't stifle a cough.

"Right." I addressed the bears. "Let's get to it."

I was familiar with the names Steiff and Gund, so I began by looking for those. Working my way around the room, I inspected labels and sorted the animals by maker, creating two piles on Linda's bed: one for Steiff, one for Gund. Before long, the piles toppled onto each other. As I sorted bears, I cleaned and dusted the bedroom, coughed, and threw away empty medicine containers and other remnants of Linda's illness.

Finally, I sensed her presence. I felt her scowling over my shoulder, unhappy I was messing with her bears, unsure what I was up to. I offered a silent apology for disrupting her space and asked for her help with this project. I couldn't intuit her response, so I continued to work.

By the time I got around to the animals on the bookcases surrounding the bed, my cough had a hacking ring. My hands were filthy. I had dust specks in my eyes, and I was pissed. These bears had been mistreated. Many were grungy and smelled of mildew. They'd been imprisoned in this apartment for years, keeping Linda company, and now she'd abandoned them.

One by one, I twisted their little, jointed arms and legs to more comfortable positions and dusted them with a damp cloth. I placed the ones without designer labels on freshly cleaned shelves. Sometimes I gave one of them an accessory or two: a necklace, a rakish hat. I placed the bears from the dirty bottom shelf on a higher one, and sat them next to friendly-looking companions. I put small animals in the laps of larger ones, leaned sweet baby bears against maternal-looking mothers.

I stepped back to survey my work. The animals appeared happier.

"Good grief," a voice in my head hissed. "Get a grip. These are *toys* for God's sake. Open a window and get some fresh air. You're getting weird."

That was it. In a flash of clarity, I understood. These were *toys*. While Linda was alive, these bears were a *collection*. With her gone, they were free to become toys again. Re-purposed into something to be cuddled. Sent back into the world as some child's lovey. I could do that.

Keeping the potentially valuable bears separate, I scooped up the others and put them into clean Hefty bags. By the time we were ready to call it quits for the day, I'd bagged over one hundred bears, puppets, monkeys, assorted rabbits and mice, all headed for a new life. While I wasn't channeling Linda exactly, I hoped I was working with her best intentions.

Now I felt more than ready for that massage.

It's Not a Bear Market

Linda's will gave us clues about where to look for help with her bear collection. It provided names and phone numbers of bear makers and collectors she'd dealt with over the years. I made several phone calls before finding Bear Maker Debi Ortega who was willing to spend some time with me culling through the collection and evaluating its worth. Debi and I scheduled a date to meet at Linda's apartment.

When she arrived, she came outfitted to work in old jeans, scruffy boots and a faded red T-shirt that read "Hugs for Bears." Her brown hair was pulled back in a pony tail and she brimmed with energy and good cheer.

Standing in Linda's living room, surrounded by stuffed animals and other accumulations, Debi didn't seem troubled. She'd been here before, delivering special-order bears to Linda. She knew the lay of the land.

"Where should we start?" she asked.

"Let's go into the bedroom, and you can educate me about this collection."

Debi surveyed the piles on the bed. "Let's start with the artist bears; those are hand-sewn by individuals who refer to themselves as 'bear makers.' Every bear maker has a brand name and a label sewn onto their product. We sell our bears on line and at Teddy Bear Conventions. That's where I met Linda."

This was a world I knew nothing about.

"I see you've separated the Steiff and Gund animals from the artist bears. That's a good start." She pulled a life-size pink pig to her chest and pressed its nose to hers. "Gunds have the cutest faces."

I picked up a large brown bear and hugged him, hopeful he might bring in a honeypot of money.

"Unfortunately, eBay and today's economy have wiped out their value."

I set him on Linda's wheelchair where he slumped and stared at us through caramel-colored eyes. He, too, seemed disappointed with this news. I gave him a comforting pat on the head.

"How much might he be worth?" I asked.

"Maybe $5. *If* you can find an interested buyer. You could try looking online. Bunch a few bears together, photograph them, put them on eBay and see what happens. It could be your new hobby." Debi offered a sly smile. I liked her.

She sorted through the bears on the bed and held out a thumb-size, tan bear with glass eyes.

"Steiff is a well-respected German company that's been making bears since the 1800s, and people are still interested in spending money on them. The value of a Steiff depends upon the color of the label. See this?" She unfolded a tiny taxicab-yellow label from the bear's left ear. "Even the tiniest Steiff will have one. The bright yellow signifies the bears were recently made. Feel this one's fur."

It felt smooth. Soft.

"Now feel this one." She handed me another Steiff. "See the difference?"

This bear, much larger than the first, had a paler yellow label. I turned his head and jointed legs forward and stroked his fur, which felt like disheveled cowlicks.

"This one's made of mohair and they're more valuable. But the *most* valuable Steiffs have white labels. They're originals, and are no longer being manufactured."

I held up a cute, chocolate-colored bear with a natty vest. "How valuable might he be?"

Debi pursed her lips. "I'm not sure. Let's call John Fort. He's a Steiff expert and is familiar with Linda's collection." Debi whipped out her cell phone and punched some numbers. "I told him I'd be here, and he said to call if I needed help." She waited while the phone rang.

"John? It's Debi. I have a question: what's a light yellow-labeled, twelve inch, mohair Steiff, in good condition, worth today?" She held the phone so I could hear John's answer.

"Not much," he drawled. "In today's market ..." He repeated what Debi told me. "But there are so many Steiffs in this collection there might be value in a slug of them together. I can come out to look, if you put them aside for me."

We agreed to do that, and Debi and I looked around for a suitable place to stash the Steiffs. We began by putting them on the recliner in the living room. Before long, it became apparent the chair could hold only a fraction of them, so we stuffed them into large Hefty bags and hauled them into the second bedroom. Soon, the pile became so unwieldy there was no room for us to move around. In the end, we bagged the Steiffs as best we could and corralled them into the oversize bathroom shower stall.

After a long morning's work, hundreds of bears, rabbits, monkeys, and assorted other animals remained to be dealt with. I knotted my hands into the small of my back, feeling daunted. I did not want to make these bears my life's work.

"What can we do with the rest that have no monetary value?"

Debi's eyes lit up. "Don't worry about *that*. There's a non-profit called Hug A Bear that distributes stuffed animals to kids in need. Would you consider donating some?"

"Let's do it." I felt cheered already.

We carried bag after teddy-bear-filled bag to Debi's car until her tiny two-seater was congested and its trunk teemed with bears. As we'd sorted, occasionally we came across animals with moth holes. We threw those into the hall, quarantining them from the others. They made a small, sad pile.

Mid-afternoon, we stopped for lunch at a near-by restaurant. No teddy bear picnic for us.

When we returned, Hanae was in the kitchen, wrapping and

boxing glass paperweights. A petite, Japanese-American woman in her sixties with a shock of white hair and a quick smile, she was one of Linda's few friends. Linda had given her an extra set of keys years earlier, and since Linda's death, Hanae often stopped to spend an odd hour sorting and packing stuff for us. She could be credited with recovering the tooth-size silver pieces stashed in apothecary jars in the kitchen. It was Hanae who unearthed the Tiffany glass vases hidden behind the sofa in apartment four, and the cameras, stacked three feet high, in the living room of apartment two.

I made introductions, and Hanae asked, "Is there anything you want me to concentrate on today?"

Debi told her how to identify the valued bears and sent her off with garbage bags to another apartment. She and I remained in Linda's apartment, bagging bears until five o'clock, when we decided we were beared-out.

"I'll come back with my truck next week and pick up more."

Debi squashed down the bears in the back seat so she could see out the rearview window, squeezed herself into her tiny car and drove off.

I went in search of Hanae, and found her poring over the pile of quarantined bears.

"What's with these?"

"They have moth issues and need to be thrown into the garbage. In fact, let's do that now so they don't contaminate the others."

Hanae held a garbage bag open and I pushed one damaged bear after another into it. There were surprisingly few.

I picked up a medium-sized bear dressed in hiking clothes. He had a blue knapsack on his back and a jaunty-looking cap. There was a brownish, quarter-size stain under his left eye, evidence of moth work.

Hanae extended the bear by his left arm. "You know ...." she said. She squinted, trying to recall something. "Linda once mentioned she'd tucked money into a bear with a zipper or something on his back. Did you find anything like that?"

Now you mention it.

I'd never considered searching the bears for hidden contraband. I shook my head.

Hanae held the bag open, and I started to drop the bear in when our eyes met. We looked from the bear to the bag and back to the bear.

Hanae's eyes twinkled with possibility. "Let's check him out."

I held his shoulders while she struggled to unbutton his backpack. She scrunched her small hand into it, and her eyes widened. She drew out her fist and opened it to reveal ... a bunch of purple artificial grapes.

"Well, at least he won't go hungry into his next adventure."

She reached in again, and a more serious expression crossed her face. This time, her fingers unfolded to reveal a thick wad of bills.

We dropped the bear and counted the money: three fifties, several hundreds, some fives, a bunch of singles. In the end, we totaled up one thousand, one hundred and seventeen dollars. We were giddy with astonishment.

Hanae held her hand to her cheek. "This guy was seconds away from the garbage can! He barely gave it up."

I flashed through the bears that drove off with Debi moments ago, given away without a thought to patting them down. Any one of them could have hidden a small fortune in his pocket or hat brim.

I hoped one of them had.

Dan the Man

Days later, when Debi drove off with the last teddy bear-filled Hefty bag, Art and I breathed a sigh of relief. We felt sure we'd made significant headway in cleaning out the apartments. We walked through them again to see the results of our labor, only to find our sense of relief short-lived.

With the exception of Linda's bedroom, living room and bathroom, no visible impact could be seen. Mechanical music machines, closets filled with musical scrolls and old clothes, computer components and screens, and copious amounts of other stuff still remained. What were a thousand or so teddy bears against so much?

We went back to feeling overwhelmed.

Art looked particularly crestfallen. "At this rate, we'll be working here until the ozone is completely torn and the ice caps are melted. This wasn't what I'd imagined our retirement would look like."

We'd been living in Mendocino when Linda died. In order to deal with the physical parts of her estate, we had to drive three and a half hours south to the Bay Area, find a place to stay and spend our days working in the abhorrent conditions inside her apartment. It was dirty, exhausting work, and we were doing it once a month. Often, we stayed with friends who graciously put up with our early-to-rise/early-to-bed schedule and provided us succor. Our workdays were long and arduous, and by the end of each, we wanted nothing more than a hot shower, a glass (or two) of wine, dinner and bed. We were not good company. Sometimes the anonymity of a hotel was easier, and we snuck in and out of town. The promise Art had made to his friend Al so long ago weighed heavily upon him.

"I think we need more than just the two of us on the job. How about asking Dan to help?" I suggested.

The room immediately took on a lighter air.

I'd met Dan twenty-five years earlier. My then-husband and I were in the midst of a bathroom remodel when our tile guy called to say he was running late.

"Would it help if I picked up the tiles for you?" I asked. The tiles had been special ordered.

"I guess." His tone was casual.

"Okay, I'll do that. So, when can we expect to see you?" My tone was casual back.

"In about three weeks, give or take."

My mood was a lot less casual at the tile store. I explained my problem to the counter person who shrugged. "So, do you want your tiles or not?"

While I was considering the question, a disembodied voice asked, "You looking for a tile guy?"

I turned and found myself looking into the blue-blue eyes of a guy with a ruddy complexion and blond hair pulled into a thinning ponytail.

"I am. My tile work was supposed to start today, but my tiler didn't show." I held out my hands in a helpless gesture.

"How big a job are we talking about?"

"Just a small bathroom."

"I could come by this afternoon and check it out."

I took a longer look at this guy. He wore shorts ending just above his knees and paint-splattered work boots. The writing on his tee shirt had been washed into oblivion.

He held out his hand. "Dan Stevenson. My truck's out back and I can deliver your tile while I'm at it."

My instincts told me Dan Stevenson could be trusted. I shook his hand, gave him my address and permission to deliver the tile.

Dan arrived exactly on time, a portent of good things.

My toddler son, fresh from a nap, was sleep-snuggly in my arms when I opened the door. He buried his head in the nape of my neck, feigning shyness.

"Hey." Dan wore the same disarming smile he had on earlier.

I rested my chin on my son's blond head. "This is Josh."

Dan held up a high five. "Hi, Josh."

Josh's shyness vanished as he slapped a high five against Dan's palm.

"I'm Dan," the tile guy said.

"Dan the Man," Josh chortled. Thanks to *Sesame Street,* he was newly fond of rhyming.

Long after the bathroom was tiled, after Dan worked for me on other projects, and years after Josh's dad and I divorced, Art was searching for a dependable tile guy. I held up my index finger. "I know someone."

It wasn't long before these two ponytailed guys with strong work ethics and educations that belied their workmen's clothing, became friends. When we thought about moving to Mendocino, Art had turned to Dan.

"I've been taking care of my friend's properties for a while, but that'll be hard to do long distance. Are you interested in taking over for me?" Art explained the scope of the job. "It could be a life-long gig for you."

Shy Linda was taken with Dan. Almost immediately she felt comfortable calling him to deal with her automotive issues, plumbing concerns, roof leaks and painting jobs. Art felt he had a clone in Dan and could leave the Bay Area with a clear conscience because Linda was in reliable hands.

Dan not only took good care of Linda's properties, he sometimes stopped by just to chat with her. Like Art, he made no judgments about her living conditions or collections or how she chose to maintain her assets. When Linda died, Dan mourned her passing.

It was Dan who came to mind now as we stood in Linda's apartment. We were sure of it: Dan would be our man.

 **Trouble**

If Dan was our right hand man, Mike Em was trouble from the get-go. A short, chubby guy with suspenders that held up droopy trousers, he reminded me of one of the seven dwarfs. Certainly *not* Bashful. Maybe Grumpy. Was there one named Sleazy?

Mike had been one of Al's mechanical music buddies. He knew everything about these instruments, including how to repair and restore them. Mike and Al had travelled together to view museum collections of player pianos, hear lectures about antique music boxes and bid for organ grinders at auctions around the country. Occasionally, they bid against each other.

Days after Linda died, her lawyer mailed her will to all the heirs. It named Art as her trustee and stipulated that after Linda's three blood relatives, Mike could select the music machine of his choice from Al's collection. That was all Mike got.

The day he received this communication, Mike called. "Art!" he barked. His voice reminded me of an impatient, yappy puppy. "When can you meet me so I can pick up my music machine?"

"You'll have to wait a bit, Mike. All heirs have one hundred and twenty days to contest the will or sign that paper you received from Linda's lawyer agreeing not to. I can't let you have anything until all heirs have signed off."

"Art, that stinks."

"Could be, but it's the law."

"I'll be in touch." Click.

True to his word, a week later, Mike called again. The message on our answering machine sounded like a line from a Woody Allen movie.

"Art! You gotta call me. I'll be at this number from ten to noon. Then I'll be at this other number until five. After that, you can call me at home. After nine, email me."

Art called him the following day.

Without preamble, Mike began his tirade. "I thought you told me I can't have my music machine until one hundred and twenty days are up. But I've been told there was a moving van at the apartment building and everything's been moved outta there."

"That's not true, Mike. Linda's sister and niece were there looking around. All of Linda's personal possessions were left to them as well as first choice of the music machines. They've sent me pictures of the ones they want. Besides, you know it would take more than one moving van to empty out that apartment building."

"My sources say they took a whole truck full of stuff."

"Your sources are wrong, Mike." His voice was calm and I admired Art's patience with this creep.

Mike grumbled into the phone and hung up.

A week later, he called again, this time with a different strategy.

"Art! I been going over Linda's will. That's not the will Al told me about. Who convinced her to change it?"

"I don't know why she changed her will, Mike. That's her business. And, please, don't call me again until the one hundred and twenty days are up. Until then, my hands are tied. Except, Mike? It might move things along if *you* signed off. The rest of the heirs already have."

Two weeks passed before Art heard anything more from Mike. Early on a Sunday morning, Mike's voice growled into the phone. "It's been rumored that you've signed a contract with a liquidator and all the stuff's going to auction. What's up with that, Art?"

"Your rumor mill is incorrect again, Mike. I can personally guarantee that you will get the musical instrument of your choice as soon as the one hundred and twenty days are up. *Or as soon as you sign the papers agreeing not to contest the will. Up to you.*"

The guy was a walking encyclopedia of drama and misinformation. After that conversation, Art began screening calls. He was relieved when he heard from Linda's lawyer that Mike Em signed the papers agreeing not to contest the will.

That same day, Art listened as Mike left a message. "Art! I signed the damn papers. When can I get my machine?"

We arrived at Linda's apartment building fifteen minutes before our appointment. Our intention was to open the four apartments to make it easy for Mike to look around. But early as we were, Mike was already on the street, pacing the sidewalk in front of a white moving van. The man behind the wheel jumped out as we approached.

Mike held out a beefy hand to Art and ignored me. "This is Shorty." He nodded toward the van driver. Both men wore coveralls, reinforcing the image I had of Mike as dwarf number eight. "He's my mover."

Art reached for Shorty's hand. "I'll open the apartments for you and you can have a look around to find —"

Mike cut him off. "What I want's in the basement."

"Then, let's have a look there." Art turned and walked to the rear of the building, Shorty and Mike at his heels. I strolled behind them and could tell by Art's gait that he was feeling cheerful. He was feeling generous. He was feeling as though his relationship with Mike Em was nearing an end.

While the men headed for the basement, I broke off at apartment four to hang out with Henry Evans, the eminent linoleum block carver and botanical print maker. Henry and his wife were personal friends of Al and Linda's. Henry had been dead for twenty years, but he was still better company than Mike.

Apartment four was filled with his prints, framed and hanging or propped against the bare wood floors, wrapped in tissue paper, and stacked in piles. A triple framed daffodil print reclined in the bathtub. At some point in the future, we would learn that there were over three thousand prints, and that would present another problem for this estate. But for now, I was happy to be dealing with Henry instead of Mike and Shorty.

I left the apartment door ajar while I worked, and noise from the basement floated up: men's voices, shuffling sounds of moving furniture, a pounding hammer, the screech of tape torn from a heavy roller. I suspected Mike and Shorty were constructing something to help them haul Mike's music player out of the building and into the van. I heard guttural heaves and low pitched grunts as a huge, wooden framed organ passed my open door. The instrument's tall, tarnished brass pipes rang out in protest as the men maneuvered it to the curb. I listened to their cautionary shouts ("Watch it!" "On your left!" "Crap, there's a step!") and waited until I heard the van doors slam and the echo of its retreating engine before I emerged.

I walked to the back of the building where I found Art locking the basement door, a smile on his face.

"How'd it go?"

He pocketed the key and brushed at his jeans. "I think we've seen the last of Mike Em."

But this assessment would prove to be premature.

The Computer Age...
Or the Aging Computer

When working on Linda's estate, we often had lunch with Dan at one of the many ethnic restaurants in Berkeley's Gourmet Ghetto. On the day Dan told us about Linda's unused medical supplies, he looked particularly pleased.

Deftly twisting thick soba noodles around his chopsticks, he gave us the update. "The Alameda County Visiting Nurses Association took everything, including the five wheelchairs and the Hoyle lift. So, what's next?"

I leaned across the table and squinted at Dan. "I think you're enjoying this."

"You're right. It's cathartic. I come from a long line of hoarders and just barely escaped. So, this is therapeutic for me."

Art plucked a pale shrimp from a steamy bowl of soup. "Then let's get you some more therapy."

Before the meeting, we'd already decided on the next project: the computers. Art popped another shrimp and told the story of how they came to be.

Al took an interest in personal computers when they first became available. He and Linda pegged them immediately as teaching tools and began developing math and science software for elementary classrooms. His natural bent toward repairing machinery led Al to learn about the inner workings of these computers, and soon, people were coming to him with their repair needs. When the school district where Linda worked decided to purchase PCs for the classroom, Al advised them to buy Commodores, at that time the most up-to-date, easiest to use processor available. His hobby turned into his new vocation: he bought a commercial building on San Pablo Avenue and opened shop. Over the years, Al mentored middle school children who showed an interest in PCs and their workings. Hanae's son Alan was one of them.

After Al died, Linda closed the shop, inadvertently encasing it in a time warp. While the rest of the world discovered Apples, Al's Commodores, aging and broken, remained in the abandoned store. Occasionally, Art would ask Linda about selling or donating them and their components, but Linda's answer was always the same: "I'll think about it." Eventually, we understood that meant, "No."

Dan slurped noodles, his eyes twinkling. "I'll round up everything computer-related in the apartments and the storage building and bring it to the shop. When it's all in one location, we'll know what we're dealing with."

"And I'll see if I can locate someone who would accept it all as a donation without charging us a small fortune to haul everything away," Art said.

For the next few weeks the men worked on their individual projects. Emails flew back and forth.

Dan: *I cleaned out Al's front office today. Dumped most of the paper work, but some stuff looked like it would be better shredded, so I did that. The front counter was filled with staplers, tape dispensers, paper punches, and random office supplies. Seems like Al's philosophy was if one is good, fifty's better.*

Art: *Nice work, Dan. And I may be onto something about the computers. I found a guy named Cliff Lewis who runs a non-profit company called* Reliatech. *It refurbishes computers and distributes them for almost nothing to low-income families. They also use old computers for job training purposes, and they're located in the Goodwill warehouse in San Francisco, so they have plenty of room.*

Dan: *I cleaned out the back office today and will make a trip to the dump tomorrow. All that's left now are tools, computer testing equipment, some model train engines and a coal car, two strands of train tracks and a little carved Japanese figure that could be valuable. But I don't speak Japanese and he wasn't talking. I'll finish off the utility closet tomorrow and take the toxic materials to the toxic waste depot.*

I chuckled as I read over Art's shoulder. "Do you think he's still having fun?"

Art grinned up at me. "I hope so. Because I wouldn't want to be doing that."

Art: *Good job, Dan. I thank you for your diligence, perseverance and fortitude. You will be rewarded. (Although maybe not in this lifetime.)*

Two days later from Dan: *A six-man, one-woman crew arrived with a forty-foot truck from Reliatech this morning. They loaded computers until the afternoon when a second four-man crew with another forty-foot truck arrived to help out. It was just them and little-ol'-me, but I was ready for them. I'd thoroughly previewed EVERY box and item, so nothing of value went out the door. They will be back for another truckload in a couple of days. Was it fun? You bet! Cathartic? Absolutely!*

I was glad to hear he was still enjoying himself.

Art: *I had a thought before Cliff picks up the rest of the stuff. Alan makes his living with computers. Do you suppose he might want any of these for old time's sake? I'll give him your phone number, if you don't mind dealing with this, too.*

The following day from Dan: *Alan called this afternoon and asked if he could send an email to his computer buddies to see if they have any interest in old computers. I told him okay. We'll get together on Wednesday. Doesn't matter if no one but Alan shows up because Cliff is coming on Thursday and it will all be GONE by the end of that day.*

Art: *Did Alan really think his friends would want any of it?*

Dan: *He came over himself just to look around and was pretty overwhelmed by all of it and by his memories of Al and Linda.*

Focused on ridding ourselves of the outdated computers, we'd lost track of the human side of this story. Hearing about Alan's reaction to being inside Al's store and warehouse brought us up short.

Later, from Dan: *A delay in plans, dude. Cliff had to postpone the final pickup because they don't have room in the warehouse for the stuff they've already taken. He assured me he would bring a larger truck and crew as soon as he distributes this last load. Have I mentioned, there's still a shitload of stuff left? Alan showed me a huge stack of boxes in the warehouse filled with computer software and thirteen PET computers. Those are heavy suckers in black suitcases with old-fashioned looking fax machines and telephones built into them.*

Art: *I'm glad it's you and not me, Dan. What about Alan's friends?*

Dan: *Today was the happiest part of this whole experience. Alan's geek friends swarmed the shop. About twenty-three people showed up and went nuts. Those PET computers were scooped up in about a minute and a half! One guy, who specifically repairs and rebuilds them, wanted them all. I called Cliff and said there wasn't as much left as I'd thought. He seemed relieved.*

Two weeks later, Dan forwarded an email from Cliff thanking us for the donation and noting that in the end, it cost *Reliatech* $532 for the crew, gas money and dump fees for the piles of binders and computer software that were no longer usable. It was a small price to pay to relieve us of this burden. Art gladly wrote a check from Linda's bank account to cover the expenses.

Back in the Bay Area, over lunch the following month, Dan made a confession. Leaning over his plate, he scooped up curried chicken with warm nan. "I'm feeling healthier, man. This unloading therapy is really working! What's next?"

16R, 24L, 37R

Art and Dan and I had been dealing with one collection after another in a fairly organized fashion. Stuff that was in our way captured our attention first. The large, steel-gray safe in the basement wasn't on our radar. We were aware of its presence, but Art was in no hurry to get to it.

Al had opened the safe for Art decades earlier and gave him its combination, which Art wrote on a scrap of paper. That paper was transferred from one place to another over the years. It was a miracle Art still knew where it was.

While his interest in the safe was lackadaisical, I was tantalized by it, imagining all kinds of treasures: estate jewelry with big diamonds, antique coins. Money. "Do you know what's in it?"

Art ticked off the possibilities. "Probably gold for Al's jewelry work. Maybe some gems. Most likely some silver. Certainly, his coin collection."

"Let's just see what's there," I coaxed. "We don't have to do anything about it right away."

Eventually, I persuaded him to take a peek.

We strolled to the basement door at the back of the building. The yard, partially paved in concrete and shaded by an old oak, was separated from the one behind it by a shoulder-high, wooden fence. An odd-shaped hole had been sawed into the fence to allow the oak's one protruding limb to grow freely. A metal sculpture stood corroding in a patch of dirt under the tree. As if in critique of the statue, the oak dropped dead leaves on it. I could see that *Sunset Magazine* wouldn't be doing a photo shoot here anytime soon.

Art put a key into the basement lock and jiggled it several times before it turned and the door creaked open. He held it for me. "This way. Be careful."

I stayed close behind as he entered the shadowy, cavernous space. He stopped just inside the doorway and plunged his arm into the darkness, searching the wall for a switch. When he found it, a series of dim, yellow lights illuminated the cellar, revealing workbenches piled high with hand tools, woodworking paraphernalia, table saws and two lawn mowers awaiting repair. If there was one of something, there were several of them. Above the benches, shelves of paint cans lined the walls. Screwdrivers and wrenches hung from pegs of the number and variety one would find in a well-stocked hardware store. Under the benches, twelve rusty-topped gasoline cans nuzzled against each other.

A narrow path ran from the basement's entrance to a second doorway. This entry was partially blocked by an upright player piano, half-draped with a blue plastic tarp. The exposed portion of the piano revealed a bucolic meadow scene in finely-etched leaded glass, a sharp contrast to the room in which we were standing. The piano's ivory keys, swollen and peeling, looked like arthritic fingers.

A tall organ stood to the right of the opening. The bottom half, an upright piano with three, claw-footed pedals. Above the keys, in ornately scripted letters, round, white-faced knobs spelled out the words *oboe, trumpet, orchestral flute, dolce flute, bassoon.*

"When this works, each of those knobs, in combination with the pedals, emits the sound of a different musical instrument." Art lifted the plastic tarp. "Al explained it to me once. He was going to restore this, although it looks like he never got around to it. Mike Em took one like it, only in slightly better condition."

Through the second doorway, we entered a storage area three times the size of the first. We were now deep in the bowels of the basement. The safe lived here, surrounded by shelves of mildewing books, outdated and dusty school supplies, jars of paint and glitter, old glass medicine bottles, stacks of newspapers and cardboard boxes. The musty air signaled a world of objects, moldering away.

The room was damp and chilly. I pulled the sleeves of my sweater down, folded my arms across my chest and focused on the safe. It looked old and substantial, large enough to hold the body of a five-year-old child. That image made me shudder. Papers littered its top, and a box of grimy, orange yarn leaned against the front of it.

Art pushed the box aside and knelt before the safe while I took up a post inches behind him. He twirled the lock twice to clear it, then dialed the numbers Al gave him years before. Sixteen right, twenty-four left, thirty-seven right. I stood in eager anticipation as he pushed down the safe's long handle.

Nothing happened.

He tried once more, this time spinning the lock back to zero after dialing in the final number. Again, nothing budged.

Several more attempts yielded the same results: nada, zip, zero. Art rose from his crouching position with a sigh.

"What now?" I said.

"Now, we find ourselves a safe cracker."

Not In the Yellow Pages

Failing to find a listing for "safe cracker" in the Yellow Pages, we called a locksmith. The woman who answered the phone at Glenview Lock and Key was familiar with the manufacturer of our safe.

"Turn the lock *five times* to the right, then four to the left, and three to the right. You pull the handle *up*, not down, to open the door."

We returned to the basement, walked through the cobwebby entrance, and once again knelt before the safe.

Art twisted the lock to zero and mumbled to himself as he worked with this new information: "Sixteen right, *five* times; twenty-four left, *four* times; thirty-seven right, *three* times." We heard a soft click. When he pulled up on the handle, the heavy metal door scraped open. Eagerly, we leaned forward.

The safe was chockfull.

Five plastic margarine tubs lined up toward the front. Lifting the lid of one, we found it filled to the brim with gold and silver-colored nuggets, the kind jewelers use for casting.

I hefted one container, which seemed to weigh over a pound, and turned toward Art. "Could this be what it looks like?"

"Probably. But we won't know until we have it tested."

The margarine containers sat in a shoebox lid, sharing the space with assorted pieces of silverware: cake servers, soup spoons, serving forks, ladles. Wedged between these were tiny, clear plastic bags filled with odds and ends of broken gold chains, mismatched earrings and gold teeth.

I cringed at the sight of the teeth. I knew jewelers traded "used" gold to assayers for shiny nuggets of specific weights, but these teeth disturbed me.

Neatly stacked to the left were five narrow, wooden containers labeled *Gordon's Cream Cheese*. Pulling one forward for closer examination, we found it crowded with tissue paper packets tightly pressed against each other. I removed one at random and unfolded the sheer envelope.

The act felt comforting and familiar. In my mind, I pictured my five-year-old self seated next to my grandfather at his jeweler's workbench, my hands cupping my knees, legs swinging in anticipation. My grandfather's fingers, red with polisher's rouge, held an onionskin-thin paper exactly like the one I held now. He unfolded the paper with great care and pushed it toward me. Inside were tiny, colored gems: crimson rubies, bright green emeralds, cerulean sapphires, white diamonds.

"I wonder if they're real," Art said.

My grandfather's workbench disappeared and I looked down at the tissue paper in my hands. Three, square-cut, green stones, each the size of a small postage stamp, glistened against the tissue in the basement's dim light. Holding one at its edge, I brought it closer. It shone crystal clear and deep green, with no visible inclusions. If these *were* emeralds, the heirs to Al and Linda's estate were going to be very, very happy. And very, very rich.

"I don't think so." I held the stone out to Art. "They're too big, too clear, and too perfect to be real. But we should have them appraised by a gemologist. Just to be sure."

Shaken from my reverie, a thought occurred. I stood and looked down at Art.

"You know, we're the only people who have access to this safe, the only ones who know about these stones." I felt light-headed, probably from getting up too fast. But maybe from the possibility we could pocket some of these treasures and no one would be the wiser.

"It crossed my mind." His voice was even, not at all conspiratorial. No larceny instincts present. He handed the green stone back to me and stood to stretch.

I took his place at the mouth of the safe and poked my head into it. Reinserting the tissue packet, I rifled through other envelopes marked South Sea pearls, golden sapphires, canary diamonds, marquise-cut rubies, jade, Australian opals. Arbitrarily, I plucked another envelope and examined its contents. Thanks to my grandfather, I knew something about gemstones.

The opals I unwrapped were poor quality and had little fire. The pearls, too, were inconsistent in color, their nacre lacked depth. Still, maybe some had value. They were, after all, kept in a safe.

Art watched me with interest. "What do you think?"

"There are so many stones, it's hard to believe they're real. Plus, I'm looking at the semiprecious stuff — the opals and pearls — and I'm not seeing any that impress me as high quality. But we don't have a jeweler's loupe to magnify them and I'm not an expert. I think we should take a sampling of these and have them evaluated."

"I agree," Art said. He leaned into the safe to pull out a heavy, white burlap bag and stood to open it. I gazed up at him in anticipation.

Inside, paper sleeves were marked *nickels, dimes* and *quarters*. Three other bags were filled with silver half-dollars. This currency might be worth nickels and dimes and quarters. Or, depending upon their condition, date and mint location, they might be worth a good deal more. Again, we didn't know.

Hidden under the last of the cream cheese boxes, a business envelope contained $1800 in small bills.

I straightened and arched my back. "We could have a nice dinner at Chez Pannise tonight."

Art gave me a rueful look that suggested he wasn't amused (or maybe not hungry) and hunkered down once more in front of the safe. He reached into the very back and pulled forward two sample cases of wedding bands, each stamped 14K. A box under them contained several chunky, crudely-fashioned gold rings.

"Al's work." He held up a tin containing an assortment of gold-colored porcupines. "These, too."

Some of the rodents were as large as a child's fist, several were larger. The quills on a few had been polished to a golden shine, most had not. Polishing gold porcupine quills is undoubtedly a tedious job and one more thing Al hadn't gotten around to doing.

Art coughed and stood up. "I've seen enough for one day. We'll need professionals to tell us what we have here."

We returned everything to the safe except for a sampling of gems and a handful of gold-colored nuggets, which we intended to have evaluated. Art turned the lock on the safe, and we walked upstairs to Linda's apartment, each in quiet contemplation of the temptations we'd seen. It didn't feel like a Chez Panisse night after all.

We found Hanae in the kitchen, seated in Linda's desk chair. Between her feet was a large box of green glass medicine bottles. She had been wrapping each bottle individually in old newspaper, but stopped her work when we came through the door.

"I was wondering where you two were."

Art sighed, as he often did when working on estate-related stuff. "We were in the basement, looking through the safe."

Hanae looked up inquisitively. "Which one?"

The Safecracker

With Hanae's direction, we located the second safe, hidden near the workbenches under a tattered rug. Art didn't know the combination of this safe, so we were forced back to the Yellow Pages to find an actual safecracker.

Gary arrived later that afternoon. I expected a wiry guy with nimble fingers, but he turned out to be solid and blond and looked like a surfer dude. For a tool kit, he carried a black case, the size and shape of a doctor's medical bag.

Art led him down to the basement and knelt with him in front of the newly found safe. Gary opened his tool kit, removed a four-pronged metal object he called a gear puller, and fit it onto the combination lock. The tool covered the lock and its prongs latched onto the face of the safe. With the expertise of a professional and the application of brute force, Gary turned the gear puller, removed the lock and unscrewed the plate behind it. Then he drilled a small hole into the plate, sending the acrid odor of ground metal into the air. The drilling completed, he grabbed another tool outfitted with a tiny light, a mirror and a magnifier. Inserting this into the hole, he peered into the mirror to see the tumbler inside the safe. As he turned the combination knob, he watched the keys inside the lock fall into place.

The good news was, it didn't take long to open the safe. The unsettling news was a smaller, jeweler's safe, nestled inside it. The two men grinned at each other.

Gary repeated the safe cracking process. When the smaller safe was open, its cavity revealed piles of white, burlap sacks. Art bid Gary goodbye before he opened these.

When he was alone, Art inspected the contents of the bags. Like the ones from the other safe, these were filled with coins in plastic envelopes and paper sleeves. Some were old and much-handled. Some sleeves were marked "buffalo head nickels." Several gold-colored jewelry boxes held quarters from the 1800s. Three large Mexican pesos felt heavy enough to actually be gold.

Now that he knew the combinations to both safes, Art locked them and came upstairs to look for me.

"How did it go?" I asked.

He scratched his forehead. "I think we're going need *a lot* of experts before this is over." He ticked off fingers. "We've already paid a locksmith. We'll need an assayer for the gold and silver, a gemologist for the stones, probably an art dealer for the Henry Evans's collection, a numismatist for the coins, some kind of expert for the mechanical music collection, and who knows what else?" He sounded glum.

"What about a magician?" I suggested, giving him a peck on the cheek. "To make all this stuff disappear."

The Many Prints of Henry E.

As a team, Dan and Art and I functioned well together. Individually, we were responsible and resourceful people, respectful of the stuff that made up the Nielsen estate. Together, we functioned as an efficient crew.

We differed, however, in our approach to the work. While Art and I were eager to be done with our responsibilities to Al and Linda and resume our normal lives, Dan saw this job as part of his therapeutic process. For that reason, he was the only one of us who whistled while he worked.

The three of us communicated regularly and made plans for what to do next to avoid a duplication of effort. After Mike Em removed his pipe organ and the computers were dispatched, we met at a restaurant near Linda's apartment and settled on new assignments.

The aroma of cinnamon-spiced, barbequed chicken and dilled yoghurt wafted around us as we squeezed ourselves into a booth in the tiny Middle Eastern diner. After placing our order, Art began:

"I need to get familiar with Linda's finances, so I'll spend this week looking through her desks and computer files."

"I'll work with the Henry Evans prints," I volunteered, "informally catalogue them and try to learn the particulars of the collection."

Dan happily undertook what he saw as the cathartic job of clearing out the warehouse.

Our projects settled, we ate heartily before going to work.

Back in the apartment, Art sat on the uncomfortable-looking, lopsided office chair at one of Linda's desks. He moved an empty cardboard file box and shredding machine under it. I gave him an encouraging pat on the back, picked up a bracelet-size metal ring that held the keys to all the apartments, the basement and the laundry room, and headed to unit four where the print collection was amassed.

Al and Linda had been both personal friends and patrons of the Evanses. Each December, they purchased a portfolio containing Henry's new work for the year. Often they bought several of these portfolios, as well as many single prints. Many. Single. Prints. Framed and unframed, matted and in butcher paper-wrapped stacks, these were strewn about the bedrooms and living rooms of every two bedroom apartment in the building. Each revealed the work of a master carver whose skilled hand cut away chunks of linoleum and left behind a block of delicate chrysanthemum petals resting heavily upon a thin stem or a graceful nasturtium, wispy tendrils reaching skyward. The colors were vibrant: oxblood, Kelly green, tangerine. I stood in the middle of the living room awestruck by the beauty of the work that surrounded me, and tried to decide where to begin.

It seemed a good idea to create a staging area, so I cleaned the top of a card table, some low wooden filing cabinets, a coffee table and a section of the living room floor. I dragged the framed prints into one bedroom and leaned them against a wall, then carried the unframed prints, batch by heavy batch, into the living room. I piled them, along with three fabric-covered portfolios and twenty-two cellophane-wrapped calendars spanning the years from 1977 to 1997, on the flat surfaces I'd cleared. I washed my hands time and again to keep the artwork unsoiled.

When the loose prints were all in one room, stacked two and sometimes three feet high, I began looking through them. To my amazement, I saw each print bore the penciled signature of the printmaker, along with a date and a series number. Some had been stored under a leaky window and sadly, deep reds and browns bled from one print into another, adding subtle color where it didn't belong. These would, no doubt, need to be discarded. But that wouldn't make a dent in this huge collection, which I estimated contained close to a thousand pieces of art. Later, I would learn from the estate liquidator that my calculations were off by slightly over two thousand prints.

I came across pieces signed and dedicated by Henry "to my friends, Linda and Al Nielsen on the occasion of Christmas, 1987" or "Happy birthday, Al." I also discovered a picture of Al and Linda with Henry and his wife Marsha, standing in front of the printing press in the Evans's Sonoma gallery. I put these aside for Linda's relatives, and decided Henry's widow was as good a place as any to start my research about this collection. Perhaps she would consider buying them back from the Nielsens' estate.

Weeks earlier, when we'd first discovered the extent of this collection, Art and I spent time on eBay trying to ascertain what a Henry Evans print might be worth. We found that a single print could range from $50 to $550, depending upon the detail of the linoleum block carving, the number of colors used in the printing process, and the number of issues in the series.

Looking at the calendars, I saw the Evans's Gallery phone number printed on the back of them and decided to see if it was still in service.

Marsha herself answered the phone.

I identified myself and told her the reason for my call. She was aware that Al had been dead for some years, and knew that Linda was in failing health. She was sorry to hear about Linda's death, but *horrified* to hear about Henry's artwork.

"How many prints did you say there are?" Her voice was high-pitched and anxious.

I gave her my estimate.

"But Al said he would donate them to museums and educational institutions." I thought I heard her sob.

"We want to treat this collection with the respect it deserves," I assured her. I didn't mention the bleeding prints.

I realized her dismay was the fear we would put this entire collection on eBay, devaluing her husband's work by its sheer mass.

"Would you be interested in buying them back?" I inquired innocently.

Her voice turned cold and haughty. "I only deal with first sales, not seconds. If a print doesn't originate from the studio directly, it is considered a second sale. I'm not interested in buying back *resales*." She pronounced the word like it was something vile. "I have no idea how you should handle this. Henry believed Al would donate these prints to public institutions."

I thanked Marsha for her time, hung up and called Linda's lawyer, who had an immediate response. "Under no circumstances can you donate any of these prints. It's Art's fiduciary duty to sell them and distribute the proceeds to the heirs."

I went back to Linda's apartment to report to Art.

Before I could get to my news, I saw worry furrowing his brow. Poring over her files, he'd found some horrifying information of his own. It appeared that none of the collections was insured. More than that, none of the real estate holdings were either. Not the two houses in southern California. Not the computer repair shop. Not the warehouse Dan was cleaning out. Not even the apartment we were standing in. Art's attention immediately shifted from cleaning out files to securing insurance.

There was so much to do, so many details to consider. One problem seemed to unravel into another. Happy Dan would soon discover this himself as he sorted through the contents of the warehouse.

On the Face of It

On the face of it, Dan had the least complicated job of the three of us. While Art and I were running into snags, he was busy cleaning out the warehouse.

The problem with the Henry Evans collection was a thorny one. Art understood he was legally obligated to sell the prints, but there were so many, it was hard to assess their value. Finding a buyer for the entire collection would present a challenge. Who would be willing to wait years to re-coupe their investment by selling the prints, a few at a time, over a prolonged period? Clearly, Marsha Evans wasn't going to help, and I felt bad worrying her about it. In addition, it seemed sad not to be able to donate at least *some* of the prints to public institutions as Al had promised. I thought about this problem in bed that night and hit upon an idea. I waited until the sun rose to share it with Art.

"How about having a private sale? We can invite only people we know, ask them to invite people *they* know and put a low price on each print, something trifling enough to encourage people to buy more than one."

I held up a finger for each benefit of my plan. "We'll be making money for the estate, not harming Marsha Evans, and getting some of these prints back into the light of day. Maybe some of the buyers would even consider donating one or two to a school or library. What do you think?"

Happily, Art agreed, and I began making phone calls to friends, giving each an appointment time and directions to Linda's apartment building. At the end of our work week in Berkeley, we deposited over $2000 into Linda's bank account from this sale. Not a huge sum, but we'd sent dozens of Henry Evans prints into the world. We'd done our part and the rest of the collection could be handled by someone who knew more about these things than we did.

Back at Linda's desks, Art made other troublesome discoveries. He'd found keys to seemingly missing cars and learned the tenant who lived in the apartment above the warehouse was seriously in arrears with her rent. Papers also indicated Al and Linda made a substantial, no-interest loan to a friend who'd agreed to pay it off in $300 a month installments. Art calculated she would be celebrating her 120th birthday by the time the loan was settled.

Then Dan called with a question: "Art, were you aware there are containers of toxins in all the apartments as well as the basement? Should I bring them to the warehouse where I'm finding more of that stuff?"

Art sighed. "What kind of 'stuff' are we talking about?"

"In addition to the old paint cans and cleaning supplies, I found two propane tanks, a large garbage bag full of what I imagine is asbestos-loaded plaster, some mason boards (probably asbestos), and photo developing acids. That's what I've discovered *so far*."

Another sigh from Art. "The Toxic Waste Center will only accept fifteen gallons at a time from any one person. Unless you want to be doing this when you're eighty, we might have to handle it differently, maybe find a professional removal service."

Dan agreed. "I'll move it all to the basement and we can deal with it later."

"Good plan."

And it might have been. But that was on the face of it.

Emails revealed more.

Dan: *I've found about fifty pounds of casting plaster in the basement. Shall I dump it? There's some other material I don't feel comfortable handling. Here's my Question of the Day: How much stuff can one being in the universe collect... and WHY?*

Art: *Don't save the casting plaster. It's too old now to be reliable. And the answer to your question is: I guess Al's hoarding instincts took over. I have no idea what he was doing or planned to do with all that.*

Al bought the warehouse three decades earlier. The building, located on a corner lot in a residential neighborhood, had been a mom and pop grocery store. Its purchase included the store's furnishings: multi-level shelving, wooden storage pallets, neon beer signs, a forklift for moving heavy supplies, and a "lollipop scale" large and heavy enough to weigh an elephant.

The first thing Al did when he took possession of this property was board up the display windows. Then he shoved the shelving and storage pallets to the walls to create a sizeable empty space that he began to fill. He brought in tables whose surfaces he covered with electronic tools, pottery kilns (three), metal filing cabinets stuffed with tax returns from businesses long defunct, a dilapidated-looking couch, the PET computers and a multitude of Commodore computer screens, boxes containing newspapers and periodicals, a variety of old telephones, a boxful of "Hi, I'm (fill in your name)" plastic badges and dozens of mechanical musical instruments, including an actual calliope.

A small parking lot hugged the rear of the building and a two-bedroom apartment filled the upstairs floor, facing San Francisco Bay. Under the living quarters were twin, single car garages, each deep enough to park two automobiles in tandem. And, of course, Al did.

A 1957 Plymouth station wagon, in junkyard condition, and a red 1972 Honda stood in one garage; two 1972 Hondas occupied the other. Nineteen-seventy-two was the year Hondas first appeared in the U.S., and had these cars been in mint condition, which they *so* weren't, they might have had some appreciable value.

Dan seemed delighted to email us about his progress: *The warehouse is coming along nicely. I left the larger musical equipment alone, and using the forklift, I brought everything else down to floor level, except the couch. I found things left over from when this place was a grocery store — cardboard advertisements, boxes of sales receipts, broken neon beer signs. I've developed a new rule of thumb for myself ... if something sits for more than a minute and a half, throw it out!!!!*

A more ominous email followed: *I found some stuff labeled cyanide. I think it's time we found ourselves a professional to deal with the toxic waste.*

Art: *By all means. Find someone local and keep me informed. Don't mess with that yourself.*

Two days later, Dan emailed his report: *The hazardous waste team came today to look at what we have. You wouldn't believe the level of toxicity we're dealing with. They said these old chemicals fall under industrial rather than household waste, and the asbestos is the least of it. That will be collected tomorrow by a certified asbestos technician outfitted in a special suit who will load it into a drum lined with an eleven-millimeter plastic liner. They also pointed out bottles of old chemicals that are highly unstable and should be moved only by a professional wearing protective clothing. The most dangerous of these is located in the last two closets in the apartment laundry room. They cautioned me not to open those doors again. There are at least six different kinds of cyanide here, and several chemicals that become extremely volatile if they get wet. It looks like Al had enough chemical shit here to run a close second to al Quaeda!*

Art picked up the phone. "Dan, you're doing a remarkable job, and I greatly appreciate it."

"This has been pretty interesting for me." Dan's usually mellow voice sounded hyper. "Who knew about this? Turns out we have chemicals that are against the law to move without being contained and packed in special drums. An Environmental Protection Agency (EPA) number has to be acquired by the estate and given to Environmental Services, the company licensed for packing and shipping such materials, before they can even be taken out of here."

"I'll get that number for you and get back to you ASAP."

Dan had more to share. "Did you know that even a drop or grain of a toxin has to be placed in its very own container and shipped to its very own spot in the hazard material waste stream? These technicians said they'd never seen this amount of dangerous stuff in a non-industrial setting before. What exactly was Al up to?"

Art expelled a snicker and shook his head. "I have no idea."

Three days later, Dan sent an email update: *The deed is done. And in addition to the cyanide and asbestos, the toxic techs found large quantities of zinc and mercury. But right now, all the toxins are on their way to Nevada, Alabama and three other states. I guess they'll be taking a vacation. I'm putting the invoice for the removal in today's mail. Peace out, bro. I'm tired.*

Art: *Take some time off. You deserve it.*

When the invoice arrived, Art saw a bill in triplicate and a formal letter stating the estate was no longer responsible for these toxic materials. The company that removed them from the apartment building and warehouse now had the responsibility for "advising the state of California and the EPA of the nature of the chemicals and the order and direction they would arrive at different waste-stream facilities as shown on the Uniform Hazardous Waste Materials Manifest, attached."

The final bill for toxic removal was $6308.38.

Aside from learning more than we ever believed we would need to know about toxic waste removal, we also learned that on the face of it, things aren't always what they appear to be.

Routine Business

After all the Plymouths and early era Hondas were located, when the desk drawers had been culled and the toxic material removed, when we felt we had a handle on the extent of the Henry Evans prints, and were confident we understood the entirety of the other collections comprising this estate (with the exception of the mechanical musical instruments), *then* we turned our efforts toward finding an estate liquidator. Someone to help us transform what was left into cash.

"Call Rick Hudson," Linda's lawyer advised. "He's honest and fair."

"Rick Hudson has a lot of connections. He'll find buyers for you if anyone can," said my friend Fan who once owned an antique store.

Another friend, Hether (yes, without an a), a self-confessed hoarder, rhapsodized, "I love going to Rick Hudson's sales. He has *everything*."

We called Rick and set up an appointment to meet at Linda's apartment.

He arrived on time and introduced himself with a firm handshake. He was a tall, well-built guy in his late thirties with an easy manner; we felt comfortable with him right away. As he described his business, I stared at his refined eyebrows that moved as if of their own accord.

We stood in the living room (because there was no place to sit) and discussed Art's responsibility for this estate.

"I'd like to get the most money I can for the heirs."

"I understand," Rick said. "I'm a third generation liquidator, and I've dealt with many estates like this. Maybe with slightly different stuff, but this is pretty much routine business for me."

My mind was racing. *Routine business? Really?*

As he spoke, he rubbed his hand over a low wooden cabinet, opened its door, and casually inspected its contents. His eyes continuously roamed the room, observant, inquisitive. He bent down and retrieved an Evans print wedged between the couch and the wall, and nodded at it appreciatively.

"That's one of a lot more," Art said.

"A lot?" Rick lifted an eyebrow.

"A living room full. Come. We'll show you." Art's tone was cheerful as we led Rick to apartment four.

Rick's eyebrows rose to his hairline as he surveyed the stacks and piles and heaps of prints. "This is an amazing collection. It'll need special treatment."

Ha! Take that for routine.

We led Rick on a tour of the rest of the building. As we walked from apartment to apartment, his hands were busy. He swiveled the free-standing, four-sided oak bookcase, leafed through a copy of *Playboy's Illustrated Works of Little Annie Fanny*, and poked into cabinets. He marveled at the collection of mechanical music machines, and chuckled when a maniacal-looking, xylophone-playing doll struck her tiny mallet to the instrument and made it chime. Opening closet after closet of player piano scrolls, Rick shook his head.

When we came to a tall, headstone-shaped item, he let out a gleeful shout. "Wow! Do you know what you have here?"

Art and I exchanged looks. Of course we didn't.

"This is a Zenith Stratosphere. Between 1935 and 1938, Zenith produced 250 of these radios. They never made them again. Just 250 of them *in the entire known world*." Rick's calm demeanor vanished; he was now animated, bending close to examine the radio carefully. "In 1935, this radio sold for $750. A brand new Ford *car* cost $650 back then. I Googled this once: in 2007, one of these sold for $72,000! There are only 40 left in the world today. And you have one."

"Really?" Art and I said in unison. We were stunned. The more so because we knew this instrument was uninsured.

Routine business my ass.

Feeling buoyant now, we led Rick down to the basement to see what other treasures he might discover.

Before our eyes had a chance to adjust to the dimly lit cellar, Rick began exploring. He walked around like Alice discovering Wonderland, looking this way and that, pausing to scrutinize the dark contents of an apothecary jar, peering into dusty boxes and inspecting the workbenches laden with tools. Near the largest of the safes, he plucked something silvery from a pile of odds and ends and held it up for us.

"Gosh. I haven't seen one of these in a long time."

We looked at it blankly. "What is it?"

"It's a frame. But, see? It's also a bookend. The guy who crafted this, I forget his name, was a famous engraver. He also etched elaborate designs into leather book covers that were placed behind the bookend and framed it. It's sterling silver and a pretty rare find these days."

I cringed. With our uneducated eyes, Art and I would probably have chucked it in the trash.

"As we clear out the basement," Rick said, his eyes still darting, "I'll keep an eye out for its mate." My confidence in him was growing.

When we finished touring the apartment building, we drove Rick to the computer repair shop and then to the warehouse in Albany. He took it all in. He didn't shake his head in wonder or lift his hands in horror or even raise an eyebrow. Art and I were in silent agreement: Rick was the magician who would transform all this into cash.

"Just one thing," Rick said. "This mechanical music collection is something I'm not familiar with. I'm going to have to do some research, which will take time. And my time is money."

Art and I exchanged a look.

"I can sell the Zenith Stratosphere for you tomorrow, probably this afternoon, with one phone call. The merry-go-round calliope, too. I know the guy who used to buy this stuff for Michael Jackson. It's something Michael would have wanted for sure."

You still *know the guy,* I wanted to say. *Maybe he has other wacko clients.*

"But you probably don't want to sell the Strat on its own and break up the collection, right?" Rick's eyebrows were moving again.

Art felt they were giving him some advice. "That's right, I don't want to do that."

Rick nodded. "That's smart. I'll have to do some research about what we have here, and I'll need to find someone to help me identify these musical instruments."

I chuckled. *'Routine business?' I don't think so, Rick.*

Photo Gallery

Linda's bedroom before the clean up.

Bears, repositioned with their new friends.

Stuffed

Living room couch before.

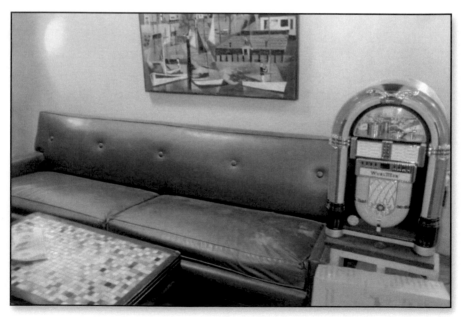

Living room couch after the bear give-away.

***Steiff bears
in the shower stall.***

***Mechanical music organ grinder
and framed Henry Evans print.***

Zenith Stratosphere Radio Model 1000-Z. Two hundred and fifty models were produced between 1935 and 1938 and originally sold for $750. Only 40 are known to exist today. This example sold for $72,000 in 2007 (photo reproduced from 8½″ × 11″ printed catalog).

Parts of the Calliope.

Mechanical organ similar to the one Mike Em took.

Organ stop knob selections.

Automata.

***Maniacal-looking,
xylophone-playing,
mechanical music doll.***

Music, Music, Music

We signed the contract with Rick, omitting the mechanical music collection. Like all the others before it, we wanted to know something about this potentially valuable accumulation before handing it over to someone else.

With everything but the music collection in Rick's capable hands, Art and I treated ourselves to dinner. We felt almost cheerful as we toasted our good fortune in finding a reliable Stuff Handler.

Art raised his glass to mine. "May this be over soon."

His tone was hopeful. We drank. Then he frowned and shook his head.

"What? Is it the wine?" I sniffed at my glass.

"No, not the wine. I was just remembering. All those years ago, after Al asked me to be the executor of his estate, he also told me it would be okay if I put a match to everything after he and Linda were gone. I assumed he was joking. Now, I'm not so sure."

"So, we're going against his wishes by being so careful with everything?"

Art shrugged. "Seems so."

We toasted again. "To Al and his Grand Plan."

Over the next week, we began our research into the world of mechanical music instruments. Starting with an online, maze-like search, one website led us to another and another. We read about music machines all over the world. Each site contained pictures of ornate and complicated devices. Most played background music created by organs with pipes or bellows, by pianos that sounded like oboes or flutes, by instruments that created music when pumped, pedaled or wound. We were treated to church recitals, boogey-woogey and ragtime concerts and music reminiscent of merry-go-round rides. It might have been a fun search ... if not for the responsibility that weighed heavily upon our shoulders.

During the first days of exploration, we came across Daniel, owner and operator of Musée Mécanique, a San Francisco museum devoted entirely to mechanical music machines.

Art explained our situation. "We're looking for someone who can identify these machines and appraise them."

Daniel asked us to email him photographs of the collection. Art scanned pictures of the calliope in the warehouse, the organs and organ grinders in the basement, the zither and player pianos in the apartments, the tin musical discs and closets of paper music rolls, the Steinway pianos, both upright and stored legless in the southern California garage. Daniel got back to us within the hour.

"Can you hear me salivating? You have some really wonderful pieces, and I would love to do this for you. But right now, I'm the only guy at the Musee. I work six days a week and my wife is threatening to leave me if I take on one more thing. How about next month?"

We were unhappy with the delay, but because he was local and enthusiastic about the project, we set a date and felt thankful we'd found a trustworthy expert.

Two days before our meeting, Daniel called. "My wife's packing her bags. She says I never spend time with her. I really want to help you, but I just can't do it now." He sounded crestfallen, and I couldn't tell if he was more upset about the collection or his wife.

For a minute, I considered asking him to call us after she'd gone, but decided that was bad form.

"Do you know someone else who could help us?"

Daniel knew no one. "But good luck." We heard the wistfulness in his voice.

Just like that, we were back to square one.

Online again, we found references to mechanical instrument auctions and demonstrations around the country. Probably the same ones Al and Mike Em used to attend. But because we had no one to guide us, and no real knowledge about our collection, we didn't pursue these.

"What about *Antique Road Show?*" friends suggested, only half jesting.

A real proposal came from my friend Fan. "Call Bonham and Butterfield in the City. They have all kinds of experts."

I made the call and listened to a recorded message. "Bonham specializes in high-end estate sales and collectables. Your call is important to us. Someone will be with you shortly." Not so shortly, I was connected to a representative.

"Mechanical music machines? You want to speak to Laurence Fischer." I was given a phone number with an international area code.

"Where would I be calling?" I asked.

"London."

Instead, I phoned the New York office of Bonham and Butterfield and received the same information. "Laurence Fischer is your go-to guy for those things. I'll give you his email address."

I emailed Laurence and scanned the pictures we'd sent Daniel. To our surprise, he telephoned us in response.

"This is *just* the sort of thing we deal with." He spoke with a crisp British accent. "My *only job* is to be on the lookout for the kind and quality of music machines you have. Your collection is splendid."

This was exciting. I motioned Art to pick up the extension.

"I am *very* interested in it and would be *de*lighted to work with you."

Yes! Art and I exchanged thumbs up.

"Viewing your photos, I'd say the entire collection might be worth $100,000 USD."

Wow! Art and I nodded toward each other with raised eye-brows, à la Rick Hudson.

"I'm sure we'll have many interested buyers at auction."

Our eyebrows lowered. *Wait. Auction?*

"How do we get these things to auction?" Art asked, his tone subdued.

"It's quite simple," Laurence said in his cheerful like-he-does-this-sort-of-thing-every-day voice. "You find an international shipping company; they'll build crates for each instrument and ship them off to us in London. After you've had them insured, of course. But first, they'll need to be appraised."

Here we were again: nothing insured in this estate, and we'd found no one who could appraise this collection. I heard the sound of gears grinding back to square one.

With both Daniel and Laurence out of the picture and no new options on the horizon, Art and I were at a standstill. Neither of us wanted to say aloud what was on both of our minds: we *had* a resource, a person who knew this collection. He was out there and more than willing to act as our appraiser. We had his contact information. All of it — his home phone, his cell, his email address.

But we just couldn't bring ourselves to discuss the possibility of calling Mike Em.

The Unthinkable Turns Into the Inevitable

Rick had casually inventoried the contents of the apartment building with us, but soon he was ready to take a more careful look at the particulars of the estate in order to organize a weekend-long, on-site, sale.

This brought us to a crisis. While Rick was eager to get on with the project, he couldn't access things that were behind, under or between the pianos, organs and music boxes. The instruments comprising the mechanical music collection were too numerous, too fragile or too bulky to move aside or work around.

The unthinkable was beginning to look like the inevitable.

We were keen to sell the collection, for sure. In order to find a buyer, the instruments had to be identified. The person who identified them would also, most likely, be able to appraise them.

But after weeks of research, we'd come up with only one person qualified *and* available to do that. Only one viable resource. And neither of us was enthusiastic about contacting him. Instead, we called Rick.

"I know a guy," Art began. "A friend of Al's. He knows this collection and he's part of the mechanical music world. He has all the right connections ..." Art paused, uncomfortable about continuing the "but" part of the sentence, and sighed deeply.

"... *but* he's an avaricious weasel, and frankly I don't want to deal with him again."

"Then leave him to me," Rick said, cheerful as ever. "I deal with these kinds of guys all the time."

There it was again: routine business.

Art gave Rick Mike Em's various contact numbers and Rick promised to get back to us as soon as he'd communicated with him. When he called a few days later, his tone was business-like, and not quite so jovial.

"I see what you mean. He's a contentious, greedy guy, isn't he? It seems he wants this collection for himself, but doesn't have the money to buy it. Also, he thinks he should have been named the executor, giving him complete access to the music machines, since he knows all about them. But, finally, when he acknowledged he wasn't the executor and he couldn't figure out a way to come up with money to buy the lot, he agreed to identify the machines and give us a rough appraisal of what they're worth. For a price of course. And — best still — he thinks he knows someone who may want to buy the entire collection."

"Really?" Art's voice turned eager.

"If you like, I'll contact this potential buyer and see if he's for real," Rick offered.

Since wheeling and dealing isn't the best part of Art's reper-toire, he readily agreed.

When Rick called again, his voice was back to its normal enthusiastic tone. "He's the real deal alright. He has money and wants to own that Zenith Stratosphere in the worst way. You should call him. But don't take his first offer. Negotiate. The Strat is your ace in the hole. Hold out for what Laurence Fischer told you the entire collection is worth. And good luck. Let me know what happens."

Enter Bob Blair.

The following day, Art had the first of what would turn into many phone conversations with Bob. Art caught him on the fly— between Europe and Florida— on his way home to Wisconsin. Bob was a very busy guy.

He had a calm telephone voice with a mild, mid-western drawl. In one lengthy exchange, he told Art he made his money, which he hinted was considerable, buying and selling large estates around the world. "I travel the continents looking for oddities and rare pieces." He confided that Al and Linda's estate was "small potatoes" for him.

Nevertheless, he was willing to have several prolonged trans-Atlantic phone negotiations with Art about the price he was disposed to pay for Al's collection. By the end of the week, they'd struck an agreement. Art surprised himself by negotiating a sound sum, keeping Laurence Fischer's verbal appraisal in mind. A contract was drawn up specifying that Mike Em was not a legal appraiser, but he would provide the photographs and instrument identification that Bob needed to assure himself that this collection was worth his money. It also stipulated that Bob was purchasing this collection for himself sight unseen.

Once the contract was signed by both parties, Bob wired a check for $50,000 to Linda's bank account. It was agreed that the remainder of the money would be transferred as soon as Bob took possession of the collection from the Berkeley apartment building and before he picked up the instruments in southern California.

The wrinkle on Art's brow eased when the bank verified the money had indeed been transferred. "But I won't feel *really* relieved until this collection is on a truck headed to Wisconsin."

Again, we were delighted to be finished with Mike Em. And again, our delight was premature.

A Flurry of Misinformation

A flurry of emails ensued in the days following the contract signing with Bob. The emails were heavily punctuated with question marks and oozed innuendo. Mike Em was at work again.

Art to Bob Blair: *Electronic transfer of funds received. I look forward to meeting you in person next week.*

Three days later, Art received an email from Bob: *I believe a ceramic cat that belongs with the Zenith Stratosphere is missing and most likely was taken by Linda's relatives. It's part of the original advertising for the Strat and belongs to the collection. Will you see that the cat gets returned? I really want it. But if it doesn't show up, we can make an adjustment to our contract.*

Art looked at me quizzically. "Do you remember seeing a ceramic cat?"

I shrugged.

Art to Bob: *I'll check with Linda's niece Robin and get back to you.*

Art to Robin: *By any chance, did you take a white ceramic cat when you packed the things you took from Linda's apartment?*

Robin to Art: *No, we didn't take anything like that.*

Art to Bob: *Robin doesn't have the cat, but I'll check further and will keep you informed.*

Art called Rick, hoping he of the professional eyes would know something.

"Oh, yeah, I have the cat," Rick said. I could see relief flood Art's face. " I took both the Strat and the cat to my warehouse for safekeeping. While they're there, they'll be covered by my insurance. I thought that was the safest thing to do."

Art emailed Bob: *The cat's been found. Rick has it under guard at his warehouse.*

Two days passed before Art heard from Bob again: *I've been told that the Aelon organ has "gone missing" in Linda's house in Orange County. If her niece has taken it, will you inform her that it is part of my collection?*

I had visions of Mike Em rubbing his hands together, gleefully, like Rumplestiltskin, intentionally feeding Bob trouble-making misinformation.

"Mike is such a creep," I said.

Art didn't disagree.

Patiently, he responded: *I'll check with Robin and get back to you, Bob.*

That same day, Art sent an email to Robin with a photo attachment of the organ in question: *Robin, have you seen this?*

Robin responded immediately: *This organ is in Linda's living room, in the same place it's been for years. Is there anything else you want me to look for?*

Art to Robin: *No, thank you, Robin.*

The furrow returned to Art's brow and I could tell he was beginning to dread checking his email. "This is embarrassing and unnecessary," he complained. "I'm not going to continue this game." There was determination in his voice. And a little disgust.

He pecked out a response to Bob: *The organ has not "gone missing." It is in the living room of Linda's house, in the exact same place where Mike photographed it several weeks ago. I believe it would benefit all of us if you stopped paying attention to Mike's fantasies and waited until you got to California to see for yourself if anything is "missing." No one is trying to cheat you, Bob.*

With a tone resembling humility, Bob wrote back: *I trust you completely, Art. I've known Mike for thirty years, and lately, he seems a little off. I will do as you suggest and wait until I see the collection for myself. Then, if anything is really missing, we can discuss making adjustments.*

There it was again, this business about "making adjustments." Art and I exchanged glances.

The computer emitted a soft ding, alerting us to a new email. We glanced at the screen. It showed a message from Mike Em.

"This should be interesting," Art said.

Art. I could imagine the bark in his voice from phone calls past. *Is there anything I can do to be helpful?*

If it were possible to reach through the computer and slap someone, Mike's cheek would be red. Art pressed *delete* and we returned to Bob's letter.

"So what do you think?" I put my hand on Art's shoulder. "Does he trust you or doesn't he?"

Art shrugged. "I'm not sure. And I'm not sure *he's* sure either."

Making Adjustments

Mike Em, troll-like as ever, was already pacing the sidewalk in front of Linda's building when we arrived to meet Bob Blair to hand off the music collection. Today, Mike wore a blue plaid shirt and baggy pants held up by turd-colored suspenders. Next to him, in Mutt and Jeff contrast, a lanky man paced in his footsteps. Mike introduced us to his sidekick, Chip. Chip nodded, but didn't remove his hands from his pockets.

Another man emerged from the side of the building in a brisk stride, his arm extended in a long handshake. "Art," he drawled. "Bob Blair. Nice to meet you."

Art introduced me.

Bob bowed his head slightly and cupped my hand with both of his. His brown eyes were lively, his tone full of cheer. "A pleasure."

I wasn't prepared to like him, but his warmth disarmed me.

He nodded toward the apartment building. "Let's go see what I bought myself."

It was obvious from the start who was in charge here — it wasn't Mike Em.

We began with a tour of the three apartments that housed the music collection. Like Rick, Bob had professional eyes. Right off, he spotted wooden crates filled with player piano rolls stuffed behind a large, oak bookshelf in one apartment. He noticed a key missing from a music box cabinet in another, and asked about a third squeeze box when he saw only two perched on the back of a faded couch.

"These come in sets of three. The smallest one is missing," he said matter-of-factly. "Mike's photos show three of them."

"Squeeze boxes don't really seem like mechanical instruments to me," Art ventured.

Bob pulled a stack of Mike's photographs from his jacket pocket and began thumbing through them. "All three are included in the contract," he said, friendly-voiced. "But if you can't find it, we can make an adjustment."

The wrinkle returned to Art's brow. "I'll ask Rick about it. Maybe he moved it." We were gathered in apartment four where the most expensive, well-maintained instruments had been stored. Bob bent to lift the lid of a beautifully crafted, inlaid music box sitting on a worn Navajo rug.

"And what about the table this music box was sitting on?" His voice was still cordial. "This sat on a small, spindle-legged table. A *music* table."

Art took pen and paper from his shirt pocket and made a note. "I'll put it on the 'Ask Rick' list."

When we finished touring the apartments, Mike, Bob, Chip, Art and I descended to the basement. Here, Mike Em entered a world of his own. He separated himself from the rest of us, and like an animal on the hunt, began to search the premises. He sniffed into musty boxes, peered behind piles of wood and paper, and poked under workbenches. His frequent refrain to Art was, "What ever happened to ... ? Did you come across ... ? Where's the collection of ... ?"

Without making any actual accusations, he sounded very accusatory. Art walked away from him and turned his attention to Bob.

While Mike continued to ferret around, Bob and Chip shifted small organs and tin player piano discs from the back of the basement to near the entrance.

Beads of sweat appeared on Bob's brow. "The moving guys will be here tomorrow and I want to have everything sorted and accessible for them."

He worked with purpose. It was clear he knew more about what now belonged to him than we did, so we stepped out of his way. From time to time, Mike called him to look at something, but mostly Bob toiled on his own, giving directions to Chip. We stayed close to answer any questions, but none arose. When Bob finished sorting, the five of us went back upstairs.

The men were given free reign to explore the collection, and spread themselves out: Chip took apartment two, Mike trolled apartment three, and Bob worked upstairs in apartment four. I had an uneasy sense about this, and conjured up the image of thieves casing a joint. However, the collection now belonged to Bob and we had little choice but to leave them to it. My hope was they weren't helping themselves to things that were *not* part of the music collection. But I realized we would never know.

Art settled himself in Linda's apartment and continued shredding old business papers. Being a less trusting person, I strolled through the apartments, making my presence known, pretending to be available for questions.

While I wandered, I admired the clean up and sorting Rick and his crew had already done in preparation for their sale. A tall bookcase in one apartment held stacks of cameras. Other cabinets were filled with typewriters, and still others contained a mass of flashlights. One bedroom looked like it had been converted into a toy store. Long tables overflowed with metal playthings from by-gone years, plastic toys with moveable parts, and MacDonald's Happy Meal give-aways.

In the living room of apartment four, I passed a table of odds and ends and noticed two glass paperweights. I wondered briefly why Rick hadn't taken these to his warehouse along with the rest of that collection and picked one up for a closer look. It was beautiful — fist-size, opalescent and etched with delicate butterflies. The other had a tangle of finely engraved ivy vines. Both were signed by the glass blowers who created them and clearly expensive treasures.

Briefly, I considered pocketing them. *Who would know?*

Besides, didn't we deserve something in exchange for all the effort we'd put into this estate? I knew Art wouldn't approve, however, and decided it was probably bad karma to consider it. I put them back where I found them and made myself walk away from temptation.

When I ambled back to Linda's apartment, I found Art on the phone with Rick discussing the missing squeeze box and the music table.

Rick's voice was loud and edgy. I could hear it clearly. "I'll look for the squeeze box, but I can tell you that table has *nothing to do with his music collection*. That's a turn-of-the-century maple entry table. I've sold hundreds of them, and never with a music box on one."

"Nevertheless," Art said in soothing tones, "we may need to let him have it. We want this sale to go smoothly."

Art went in search of Bob.

His tenor was friendly when he found him. "Rick says the table is really an *entry* table and not part of the music collection."

Looking up from his work, Bob almost hid his displeasure. He pursed his lips and frowned. "I suppose we can make some sort of adjustment about that."

This adjustment business was beginning to rankle me.

At noon, we stopped for lunch. Over drippy hamburgers, Bob entertained us with stories of his world-wide escapades selling and trading mechanical music machines.

"I already have a buyer for that Weber piano. Next week it'll be on a ship headed to Belgium where it was originally made. I hope we get it on the boat in one piece." He chuckled. "And the automata has been sold to a German collector."

I wiped my chin with a soppy napkin. "Automata?"

"The cabinet with the wooden musicians."

I recalled the cabinet. Its deep shelf held a wooden conductor and six painted musicians. The figures stood eight inches tall, and each musician held an instrument: an oboe, a flute, a clarinet, a violin, a squeezebox, and a percussive. The maestro poised a baton.

"When we get back to the apartment, I'll show you how it works." Bob's excitement was palpable. "Automata are really cool. I just finished taping a segment about them in Florida for the History Channel."

Bob's enthusiasm appealed to me. His eyes sparkled when he smiled, he had a full head of silver hair and his unlined face belied his claim to social security. I liked him in spite of the heavy negotiations he'd put Art through earlier.

During the meal, the men shared stories about how each of them came to be collectors of these unusual instruments. All found the roots of their passion in early piano lessons.

"When I was ten, I took lessons from a very rigid teacher," Mike said. Ketchup puddled at the corners of his mouth.

"Me, too," Chip nodded. I was surprised by his rich, baritone voice. "I was a poor student and didn't much enjoy the piano."

"A friend dragged me to a furniture store to see a nickelodeon." Mike spit hamburger around his words. "It was huge, much bigger than those early juke boxes, and it played all kinds of music, not just piano. That was it for me. I never took another lesson after I heard what that machine could do."

Bob told a similar story. "When I was ten, I saw my first player piano. It produced music I knew I'd never master." He bragged about deals with nickelodeons and player pianos he'd recently sold at auction for "a few million dollars" to people who "remain unaffected by the recent economic downturn."

When we returned to Linda's after lunch, Bob demonstrated the automata. He wound the device's long-handled crank, bringing the little musicians and their instruments to life. The maestro waved his baton, and pleasant, although somewhat tinny music, emerged from the machine. It was a delight.

When the show was over, the three collectors went back to sorting and packing, Art resumed his shredding, and I returned to roaming aimlessly.

In apartment four, I passed the table where earlier I'd coveted those paperweights. I stopped to have another look at them. I thought I'd remembered where they were, but I couldn't find them among the objects scattered about. I inspected other tables in the room, but it was clear they were nowhere to be found. Bob Blair was the only one packing this apartment and he instantly became much less attractive to me.

I stood in the living room, heard him moving about in the bedroom, and headed there without pausing to consider what I might say. Livid that he would take advantage of the situation, I took this as a personal affront. Did he think we wouldn't notice? (In fact, we probably wouldn't have if I hadn't considered pinching those paperweights myself.)

A little fire of self-righteousness burned inside me. Standing silently in the doorway, I watched him, my fury smoldering.

When I finally spoke, my voice was very calm. "You know, Bob, Rick took the rest of the glass paperweight collection to his warehouse. He'll notice those two are missing ... the same way I did."

Bob's hands never stopped wrapping. "They're probably in one of the boxes I packed in the living room. I'll see if I can find them."

I would have stared him down if he'd looked up. But he didn't. He just kept packing.

"In no way are they part of your music collection," I said to his downturned face. Without looking back, I walked out of the apartment.

Minutes later he caught up with me. "I found them," he said. His tone was conversational, like he hadn't just been caught stealing. "They're back on the table."

He retreated to his work, and it felt unseemly to follow him to check on the veracity of his story. But I reported it to Art.

Art rubbed his eyes. He looked tired. "Maybe that's what he meant by 'making adjustments.'"

Weeks later, after the on-site sale, I asked Rick about those paperweights.

"No, I don't remember seeing them," he said.

Then Art received an email from Mike Em. Informative as ever, he thought we'd like to know that Bob Blair had suffered a heart attack en route to Europe. "He's had quadruple by-pass surgery."

I looked at Art and shrugged. "Karma seems to have made its own adjustment."

Nearing the End

Twenty months after Art assumed responsibility for Al and Linda's estates, we were down to dealing with bank accounts, securities, five real estate properties and the mineral rights to one pesky piece of landlocked property in Fresno. We were nearing the end of our journey.

The actual *stuff* — the teddy bears and cars and musical instruments, clothing and rugs and botanical prints — was gone. Evaluated and appraised, sold, donated, recycled or — dare I say it? — dumped.

The cars with missing keys and keys with missing cars were accounted for and sold. The early Hondas, all in poor condition, were claimed by Honda aficionados with dreams of restoration.

A Navajo expert appraised the rugs and found only one of significant value. It sold at Rick's warehouse auction for $2500. My friend Fan bought a couple, and the rest were part of the two-day sale Rick held at the apartment building.

The gold really *was* gold, except for the remarkable porcupines, cast from some mysterious base metal. The actual gold and silver nuggets were assayed, weighed, exchanged for cash, and deposited into Linda's bank account.

The apothecary jars and medicine bottles that did not contain suspicious liquids and had not been transported out of state by the toxic waste professionals, were sold, over time, in batches at Rick's monthly estate sales. Collectors were thrilled to find those remarkable specimens of bygone pharmaceutical days in such good condition ... and in such quantity.

The coins, for the most part, were worth only their face value. A few of the buffalo head nickels were valued slightly higher. Three Mexican, gold, fifty-peso coins were estimated to be of real worth, and we gave those to Linda's sister. The numismatist declared the 1879 quarters "low grade" and each sold for $80.

The Henry Evans collection was purchased in toto by our friend Hether. She and her business partner attempted to contact Marsha Evans without success. Hether inventoried the three thousand plus prints and purchased a special cabinet to store them. She is treating the portfolio with great respect and considering how to best market the prints with an eye toward patience.

The gems? They were no more than I suspected. The emeralds, rubies and diamonds were either color-enhanced by heat and very poor quality stones to begin with, or laboratory-created and not worth the space they took in Al's safe. They were sold by the hundreds for $30-$60 per lot, barely enough to cover the cost of dinner and wine at Chez Panisse.

After the sale at his warehouse, Rick presented us with an accounting. Twenty single-spaced pages in two columns, enumerated the contents of the Nielsens' estate. Leafing through the sheets, we discovered the six-foot long, wooden slide rule sold for $300; someone paid $150 for Al's awful backyard metal sculpture. A laundry wringer went for $20, a broken neon sign for $65, a bag of marbles for $20, and a silver parasol handle brought in $75. An "as is" violin sold for $25. There were lists of cameras, lenses and viewfinders from every well-known camera company in the world. All of them sold. The lollipop scale went for $650. Five lots of glass paperweights — not including the two Bob Blair lifted — fetched $5000, while a glass eye brought in only $30. I thought I'd become immune to the oddities of this estate, but the glass eye caught my particular attention in a gruesome way.

A bright note arrived with the disposal of the properties. Linda's sister was deeded the two houses in Orange County, as is. We had no cleaning or sorting to do there once the musical collection was removed by Bob Blair. She immediately turned one over to her daughter, the long-suffering Robin. What she does with the other is none of our concern.

The buildings in the Bay Area were not prime properties, more like Baltic or Mediterranean Avenues rather than Boardwalk or Park Place. Each sold quickly and Hanae's son Alan was able to purchase Al's warehouse with his share of the inheritance. He hired Dan to help him clean the building and get it back in usable shape.

When Art and I were recently in the area, we cruised by. The building had been painted an attractive cream color, the boards over the display windows replaced by double-paned glass, and the shredded curtains in the upstairs apartment swapped out in favor of modern, narrow-slatted blinds. The place looked almost spiffy.

"Slow down," Art said. "I want to have a look."

I eased up on the accelerator.

Art leaned forward as we drove past. "Go around the building again."

I circled the block, found a parking space in a red zone and waited in the car while he got out to have a closer look. He cupped his hands around his eyes and pressed his nose to the new, darkly tinted window.

When he returned to the car he was shaking his head and smiling.

"What?" I asked.

"The space looks clean and empty except for new chrome shelving which hasn't been pushed against the walls yet. In one of the windows there's a huge, rainbow-shaped bridge made out of red Legos."

I raised my eyebrows. "But the shelves are empty, right?"

"Right."

"And there are no apothecary jars around?"

"Nope."

"No Henry Evans prints?"

"Not that I could see."

I narrowed my eyes. "Alan hasn't asked you to be the trustee of his estate, has he?"

"Not yet."

I pressed my foot to the accelerator. "Good. Then let's get outta here."

 **Grace**

We experienced a moment of grace just before Art wrote the final distribution checks to the heirs, of which he was one.

The outstanding balance of a loan Al and Linda made to their friend Helga was years from being paid off. Helga had borrowed the money for a down payment on a house two decades earlier. She had adhered to her agreement to pay it back in $300 a month installments, and she had never missed a payment.

But over the years, Helga's health deteriorated. She was living with a diabetes-related foot problem, was legally blind and surviving on disability checks. Her home was her only refuge and possession of value.

In order to close out the estate, Art needed to come to terms with this loan.

"I'd like to forgive it entirely," he told Linda's lawyer.

"Legally, you don't have the authority to do that," she shot back.

"What if I got all the heirs to agree? We would each be giving up a portion of our inheritance."

"You could try." She didn't sound hopeful.

He did try and this is the letter Art wrote:

Before I can finally close out the business of this estate, there is the balance of a loan Al and Linda made to a friend in the amount of $32,000. This friend has been faithfully making monthly payments, but it will be years before she will be able to pay it back in full. She is in poor health and living off disability *checks. In the spirit of Al and Linda's generosity to us, I am proposing that each of us relinquish our share of this loan. Please let me know as soon as possible what your decision is.*

Within two days, Art received his answer. All the heirs agreed to forgive Helga's loan. Writing to Helga to tell her this news, Art felt like he was participating in a blessing.

 **Epilogue**

Well over two years have passed since we first stepped across the threshold into Al and Linda's world and began the chore of disbursing their estate. It's been a journey of discovery and instruction, frustration and dedication, and disturbance on many levels.

This duty that Art agreed to when he believed his friend would never die took both our time and patience. We spent hours traveling to the Bay Area to work amongst grimy, mildew-y possessions, sometimes with interesting and/or unsavory characters. Art devoted hours to banking details, email and paper correspondence, accounting and tax information. Often, our dining room table was cluttered with the business of this estate.

Rummaging through and having to dispose of Al and Linda's possessions has had a profound impact upon us. Art says he'll never again act as anyone's trustee (although, in fact, he's already agreed to play that role for his 94-year-old Aunt Doris).

For my part, I discovered something important about my own procurement habits.

Like Al, I enjoyed the sport of shopping: hunting down my prey, fixing it in sight, capturing it with my credit card, bringing it home and displaying/using/wearing it with pride and satisfaction. I always understood that portion of my acquiring experience. My new insight has to do with the other end of it. The letting go.

Since this experience, I've created a mantra for myself, kind of an Equation of Possession. *Bring stuff in, send stuff out.* For every new item I carry into our house, I've committed to taking something old out.

Turns out, there's great satisfaction for me in sending things back into the world to be useful to someone else. Linda's teddy bears were the first to show me the way. Now, I apply that lesson to my own stuff.

And finally, it's come down to this...

We Acquired From the Estate:

* 3 two-inch tall, cobalt blue bud vases (They sit on a shelf in our dining room where we admire them daily for their beauty and tenacity to survive, intact, amongst all that other stuff.)

* a jarful of quarter-size, fused glass discs (We've made some of them into necklaces and given them to friends.)

* 1 sample casting (Art uses this to show to his clients who are interested in the process of lost wax casting.)

* 2 Henry Evans prints (Now professionally framed, they hang in our living room.)

* 1 small teddy bear (When you turn him on, he wiggles his ears and sings *Wild Thing.*)

What We Didn't Acquire:

* any other teddy bears

* apothecary jars or medicine bottles

* collectable coins

* new plaid shirts or still-in-their-original-packaging white cotton socks

* Navajo rugs

* tools

* camera equipment

* old cars

* exotic radios

* mechanical musical instruments (Although I did have my eye on that maniacal-looking, xylophone-playing doll.)

We Learned That ...

* When you say *yes* to being someone's executor, don't count on them not dying.

* A hot shower after a day of working in repulsive conditions is more than necessary — it's therapeutic.

* A Health Care Directive is not enough to support anyone's final wishes. Everyone needs to have a *face-to-face conversation* with their primary care physician when they're healthy and sane to let him/her know what their end of life plan is. Family and friends need to advocate to support that, *especially* if it looks like a patient's judgment is impaired. Make a specific provision in a durable power of attorney that spells your wishes out in black and white. Then hope for the best.

Insight I Gathered Along the Way:

* Art and I function well as a team.

* Art has great patience and integrity.

* The organization gene I inherited from my mother is invaluable and I thank her for it.

* A paper trail of correspondence allows for a good night's sleep.

* Watching meals prepared on the Food Network Chanel is a lot less fulfilling than sitting down with a good friend and sharing a meal.

* The rule of Supply and Demand applies to art as well as the world of economics.

And ...

* in the end, it's all about relationships. The rest is just stuff.

I want to acknowledge, first of all,
Linda and Al Nielsen who allowed us access to the
eclectic remains of their lives and without whom
this book would not have been possible.

Acknowledgments

I offer additional and heartfelt acknowledgements to:

Dan (The Man) Stevenson III whose stick-to-it-iveness calmed us and strengthened our resolve to press on and complete the onerous task of dis-assembling the Nielsen estate.

Warm gratitude and hugs to our friends Jo and Norm who provided succor at Chez Budman during this arduous journey.

Many thank yous to my Thursday night writing group, the Write Women — Molly Dwyer, Fran Schwartz, Amie McGee, Judy Summers and Alena Deerwater — for their keen editing eyes and for slogging through the debris with me chapter by chapter, week after week.

Thank you, my friend Katy Pye, for finding just the right title for this book. My appreciation also extends to writer, teacher, anthologist Victoria Zackheim for encouraging me to "Write on!" and to Suzanne Byerley, my final editor, who first identified these scattered chapters as a "manuscript." Her untimely death leaves a hole in the heart of our Mendocino writing community.

A big bow of appreciation goes to my husband Art Weininger for his patience throughout this entire process. As he often said when we were plowing through yet another collection in yet another storage space, "I think I see a light at the end of the tunnel ... and I don't believe it's an oncoming train."